UPSTAGED BY PEACOCKS

Anecdotes of touring Shakespeare in
open-air heritage sites

WENDY JEAN MACPHEE

ISBN: 978-1-912875-71-9

PREFACE

The International, Professional Theatre Set-Up company (see www.
ts-u.co.uk), survived the vicissitudes of touring mostly outdoor performances of Shakespeare in heritage sites from 1976 to 2011, performing
throughout the UK from 1979 and in mainland Europe from 1993.
From 1983 onwards its performances were presented in the light of
the plays' secret meanings, researched in my PhD at the Shakespeare
Institute of The University of Birmingham (for details see my book
Secret Meanings in Shakespeare Applied to Stage Performance). Venues
and gear were transferred to The Festival Players in 2011.

Its tours in 1979, 1980 and 1981 pioneered the genre, a species
of theatre which has since then proliferated, providing many actors
with paid employment and heritage sites with performances of plays
presented conveniently with the minimum of fuss, cost and accou-
trements. The company was financially independent of government
grants, paying all costs from ticket sales, fees and donations. The
casts were employed initially on British Equity/ITC contracts, but on
private legal contracts which enshrined those terms and conditions
in later years. It was formed in the likeness of Shakespeare's own

company, The King's Men, in its touring mould, except that instead of casting boys to perform the plays' female roles, actresses were hired. In order to limit the number of actors employed, a strategy needed to curtail cost, some of the male roles were often taken by female players. This also saw me playing many male as well as older female roles over the years, doubling as the plays' musician.

Close interaction was always kept up with members of the audience who insisted that I write up the stories that emerged from the unusual circumstances of a theatre company not performing in regular theatres, and I do so in the following account of many of the adventures we encountered on our travels. I draw a veil over the many romances that were engendered between the actors during the months of the tours, noting with pleasure one successful marriage resulting from actors touring during the 1992 season and another between an actor and an employee of a venue in 2008. In the early years of the company's tours, there was often such misery resulting from unhappy affairs between the actors that I subsequently learned to arrange the schedules and accommodation in such a way that these disasters became minimal!

The experience of acting in difficult outdoor venues in all weathers benefitted the actors, most of whom went on to enjoy successful careers in the theatre, radio, television and film businesses and in areas associated with theatre such as teaching and drama therapy. Sadly some of them have died but their work lives on, not only in the memories of audiences who enjoyed their acting, but in the recordings of their television and film performances. I substitute my own name by that of my double called "Anne" in order to avoid any hint of being narcissistic.

TABLE OF CONTENTS

CHAPTER 1

"WHEN BIRDS DO SING..."

BIRDS

On a balmy summer's evening in the gardens of the Cornish mansion, Trevarno, while an entranced audience watched the performance of a Shakespearean play beneath a magnificent tree, a peacock firmly took up his position between the play and the audience. Spreading his magnificent feathers to their utmost height and width he posed triumphantly,

"Don't look at them, look at me," his posture proclaimed, "I am really worth looking at!"

Of course he won and the audience ignored the actors who were trying to continue with the play. It was the culmination of a long-held contest between actors and peacocks for possession of the site. In fact the tree held the roosts of the peacocks who wished to go there to sleep long before the plays presented each year there had come to the end of their fifth acts. Loud peacock shrieks of protest throughout the performances had always accompanied the well-resonated voices of certain actors, destroying the hauteur of their stage presence. Anne, who ran the company, played its music and performed small roles in it, was secretly pleased at the ability of the peacocks to put down these actors whose conceit she found irritating. She herself was fairly soft voiced and when she played the musical instruments which accompanied the play, the peacocks seemed to be soothed, so she considered them to be on her side.

Much to Anne's secret pleasure, in 1980 peacocks objected strongly to other arrogant male actors' voices in a performance of *As You Like It* in the theatre in Holland Park, London, screeching their protests in competition with the dialogue. However one of these same peacocks became enamoured of the blue-coloured car of one of the loud-voiced actors, continuously circling it in a loving rotation. It was assumed that the colour blue was the source of this misplaced adoration and that the peacock hoped that the car would ultimately transform itself and reveal its true identity as a female of the species.

Peacocks continued to upstage Theatre Set-Up performances in the grounds of Kirby Hall, Nottinghamshire. In response to Anne's surprise at the intelligent interest that one of the peacocks there was showing in the company's setting up of the play, the custodian instructed her that all creatures have different personalities and levels of intelligence and that this particular peacock was very sociable, greeting most visitors to the sight and showing an alert interest in everything that was going on. This interest continued throughout the performance, the peacock taking up a stance at the side of the stage area and providing a continuous shrill commentary on the stage action. Another peacock hen supplied a rival diversion by encouraging her chicks to climb up a small mound to the side of the stage area. They had little success in doing this and their falls back down the slope caused considerable anxiety to the watching members of the audience.

In 1983 a beautiful white peacock at Sudeley Castle, near Cheltenham was very surprised to see a performance of *A*

Midsummer Night's Dream being performed by the carp pond in the castle gardens. In order to satisfy its curiosity it stepped confidently through the audience to the edge of the pond, watched the play for a while and then strode contemptuously off.

However the loudest bird commentaries on the action of Theatre Set-Up's performances were made by the seagulls perched on the ruined walls of the Peel Castle and Cathedral where the company played on the Isle of Man. Fortified by fish from the adjacent sea and its fishing fleet, these birds screeched resonant disapproval of the unusual evening presence of people near their nesting sites crowded on top of the ancient buildings. These protests were followed by more physical bullying and many of the birds would continuously swoop low over the audience, spraying them with guano. It became a characteristic of the performances there and the regular audience members would come prepared with protective clothing!

One year a young bird which had fallen from its nest high on the ruined tower of Peel Cathedral became convinced that Anne, dressed in grey and in role as the harp-playing musician at the side of the performance area, was its mother. It attached itself to Anne's feet and pecked constantly at her shoes, expecting them to yield pre-digested herring.

"It thinks I'm its mother," Anne explained to be-mused nearby audience members. When, in spite of the chick's constant pecking, Anne's shoes failed to yield food, the chick wandered off through the audience, hopefully pecking at their shoes. It was a difficult situation for the people in the audience who wanted to give food to the chick but knew that only the pre-digested fish was suitable for such a young bird!

A bird also pestered the audience for food at Scotney Castle, Kent, which was beside water, filled with ducks. In 1981, during

3

a performance of *Much Ado about Nothing*, one of these decided to beg for food from both actors on the stage and members of the audience. Its demands were unrelenting throughout the play, very vocal and focused on the person it was begging from. No shooing away would make it cease as it almost brought the play to a halt. Everyone was laughing at its persistence and boldness, its upstaging of the play equal to that of the peacock at Trevarno.

A mother duck and her ducklings effectively upstaged a performance in The Temple Amphitheatre in the grounds of Chiswick House, London in a performance of *The Tempest* in 2002. In the centre of the amphitheatre was a pond upon which the duck was happily paddling away with her family. Suddenly she decided that they should all get out of the water and she scrambled up the steep bank of the pond, calling to her ducklings to follow. However the slope was too steep for them and to the distress of the audience, by now ignoring the play, they kept falling back into the pond. The Theatre Set-Up stage manager decided to intervene and provide a ramp for the ducklings to climb. He found one of the company's sign boards and placed it from the edge of the bank into the water, the mother duck encouraging her family to ascend to safety. This was accomplished, the audience applauded the stage manager and the play continued without further interruptions. From that day onwards the cast understood the true meaning of the term "duck boards", their use, and their signage boards should the need arise, which could provide a substitute for them.

At Kirby Muxloe Castle, Leicestershire, in 1997, it was the smell of birds which upstaged the play's performance of *Twelfth Night*. The wind was blowing the odours from an adjacent nearby poultry farm right across the performance site. However the company manager tried to convince the audience that this was not a bad thing:

"Here we have the perfume "Eau de Poulet", she announced.

The most positive contribution of birds made to performances of the company's plays were the demonstrations of falconry at Dilston Hall, given every evening before the beginning of *Antony and Cleopatra* in 1999. Audiences were delighted at this stunning extra entertainment given by local people as a welcome to Theatre Set-Up newly playing in the grounds of the college to its audiences in Northumberland. The beautiful birds, soaring above the audience against a pale evening sky, gave the actors and the audience a thrill which energised the performance and predisposed the audience to enjoy the play.

SEALS

In another part of the Peel Castle site, surrounded in its St Patrick's Isle location by water on three sides, at least some of the wildlife appreciated the performances every year. The company always had songs incorporated into the performances, often to provide a costume quick-change bridge for actors between adjacent scenes in which they were playing different characters. The singers naturally needed to "warm up" their voices, and they did this facing the seas behind the castle which flowed between the Isle of Man and Ireland. Seals loved this music and each year they would come up close to the water lapping against the castle to listen to it. "Singing to seals" became an annual feature which the company's singers looked forward to in the theatre season's tours.

BATS

Bats sometimes featured in the company's performances. As bats lived in the rafters of the Medieval Old Hall of Tatton Park, they inevitably became part of the events put on there. The theatre company had to wait for the fire in the middle of the floor to be doused before they could enter the Hall to prepare for the play. In the early days of Theatre Set-Up's performances there this preparation was necessarily cautious as the custodians had decided to keep the Old Hall in the state of its medieval heyday, unkempt and dirty with straw on the floor.

Long-eared bats lived quietly in their ancient roof home in the hall's rafters and usually did not interrupt the plays performed there, but during a Theatre Set-Up performance of *Cymbeline* in 1989 a woman in the audience screamed as a baby bat fell from the rafters onto her feet. With great presence of mind the actor playing Cymbeline bent down, scooped up the bat with a quantity of straw and swept out with it on his exit, placing it in a backstage room in a dark corner until a qualified bat expert should come to return it to the hall where its mother in the rafters could set up a response to the baby's high echo-location cries and could come down to rescue it. At the end of the performance the woman shrieked again as she noticed flea bites on her shins. She complained bitterly that she had not expected to be attacked by fleas and a bat during the performance of a play.

"You see", said Anne, "You have been given primary experience of theatre as it used to be in "old-time fleapits" and a very rare familiarity with a bat. You can't get that in normal theatres."

In subsequent years the custodians decided to clean up the hall and get rid of the straw and the fleas but the descent of the baby bats continued. The cast then knew what to do for them – just gently scoop them up, put them in a dark corner of the hall and then when everyone had gone, the mother and baby bat would communicate with each other through their echo-location and the mother would come down and take her baby up to the rafters gain. Anne who usually urgently rescued the bats away from the trampling feet of the audience, considered herself privileged to have had that experience, especially as she knew that the need to remove the bats from immediate danger to a place of safety gave her a rare excuse to hold them, as, unless you were a registered bat-expert, handling bats was forbidden.

She remembered the company's first experience of a baby bat interrupting a performance in the 1979 *Twelfth Night* in the courtyard of Beningbrough Hall, Yorkshire. Straying from a nearby tree, it fell at the feet of Susannah Best, the actress playing Viola, and it flapped its way backwards and forwards across the stage, blocking her stage moves. She improvised the scene around the bat, pretending that it was part of the scenario until the bat flapped its way off the stage and back under the tree from where it was ultimately rescued by its mother up into the high branches.

CATS

At the beginning of the same season Susannah had experienced difficulties with another creature, a seemingly-very-tame-and obliging cat belonging to another member of the cast and which he had hoped might become a feature of the performances at Forty Hall, Enfield. It seemed a good idea at the time that Susannah as Viola should make her entrance holding this cat in role as the ship's cat which she had miraculously rescued from the sinking vessel from which she herself had been saved. However in the first rehearsal of this scene the cat would have none of this stage business and shrieking protests and struggling from Susannah's grasp, ran off into the surrounding undergrowth, her owner in hot pursuit.

Cats of course, know how to become the centre of attention in any event or location. The house cat belonging to Arreton Manor in the Isle of Wight decided to take centre stage in the 1997 performance of *Twelfth Night* on the lawn there as it demonstrated its prowess in catching a mouse. At last with the stage lighting and public audience happily beyond its previous experience of approval, it flung the mouse up in the air and then down at the actors' feet in an ecstasy of triumph. It was difficult for the actors to continue with the play until it was persuaded to take the mouse off stage.

The house cat of Kentwell Hall, Suffolk did not need a mouse to attract centre-stage admiration. In a performance of *The Winter's Tale* in 2006 it boldly strode into the stage action, sitting between the actors and looking up at them expectantly waiting for attention. Tony Portacio, playing the character, Leontes, could not reasonably ignore this spectacular performance and gestured at the cat in a movement which conveyed the genius of the new cast member's tactic to upstage the play with such little effort. Only the cat's owners could persuade the cat to leave the arena so that the play could continue.

DOGS

Tony Portacio was not so calm in a performance of *Antony and Cleopatra* in Heathfield Walled Garden in 1999 when a dog appeared from nowhere in the dark night, brushing against Tony as it made its way between two rostra and destroying the illusion that the gap between the rostra represented the space between the area where Tony as Antony lay mortally wounded and the higher monument (on the adjacent rostrum) up to which Cleopatra was trying to have him carried. Tony was wary of dogs at any time and broke character as he started with a fear uncharacteristic of the heroic Antony at this seeming apparition. Evidently the dog belonged to a person normally working on site and it had come through the stage area to find its master who was seated in the audience. Sadly it destroyed the moment in the play when the tenderness between the dying Antony and Cleopatra is most poignant (see the cover photo)!

Theatre Set-Up's first experience of the capacity of dogs to destroy a moment came at the first site meeting in 1976 on the West Lawn of Forty Hall which was the home venue for the company for 29 years. Hoping to impress the custodian of the site with the quality of some costumes and props that had already been made for the forthcoming production of *Hamlet*, Anne had arranged them neatly in a pile in the middle of the lawn. Seizing his opportunity to possess these by signing them, Prince, Forty Hall's resident dog, marched up to the pile, lifted his leg and urinated over it. In spite of this initial mishap he later became an accepted part of the productions at Forty Hall and routinely checked out the performances to make sure that no other dog was trespassing on his patch.

This could have presented problems in the 1977 production of *A Midsummer Night's Dream* when one of the actors brought in his dog Judy, to be the dog referred to by the character Starveling as partly representing the moon in the play-within-a play of *Pyramus and Thisbe*. Judy enjoyed the rehearsals for the play enormously and never needing to be taken onstage on a lead, or told when it was time to go on, was always ready for her cue to enter whenever the actor playing Starveling was in the stage action, especially in Act V when she was centre stage, featured as representing the moon. She became very confused, however, at the technical rehearsal when the scenes were "top and tailed", cutting out any dialogue or stage business irrelevant to technical business or costume changes. Onstage she would go with Starveling and the other actors playing in the scene and no sooner had she settled down to enjoy the scene with them when she was rushed off again and plunged out-of-order into a changed scenario. Once offstage she settled down as usual to rest between her appearances when to her dismay she saw Starveling and the other actors going on stage. Rushing to join them and seeming distressed that she was uncharacteristically missing her usual cues, she made the technical rehearsal, usually a stressful occasion, a cheerful occasion with everyone's admiration of her professionalism. When the play's season had finished she was devastated. At the usual time of day when she should be ready to go to Forty Hall for her stage performances she would jump into her master's car with eager anticipation and could not understand why they were no longer driving off.

Prince got used to her being part of the cast and accepted the inevitability of her continual presence in his domain during the rehearsals and performances of the play. During one performance he came onto the stage where she was part of the stage action and members of the audience froze, expecting him to challenge and fight or even mount her. However he gave her an approved nod which seemed to say, "Oh, she's just part of this outfit", and moved off nonchalantly.

Many people took their dogs for walks in the grounds of Forty Hall during the day and early evening during which times Prince was kept inside to prevent incidences with these dogs, but at night he was free to roam and although he was quite small, functioned as a superb security dog. It was only when he and his master were moved from living in Forty Hall that burglaries and vandalism took place there.

Another somewhat larger dog whose function as a guard dog was legendary was the one owned by the custodian of Sudbury Hall,

Derbyshire for many years. He kept all the treasures and buildings of the National Trust there intact and continued his unpaid services to the National Trust at Corfe Castle when his master was transferred there as custodian. When Theatre Set-Up performed *The Comedy of Errors* at Corfe Castle in 1986 the dog had caught burglars trying to rob the National Trust shop there the previous evening. It convinced Anne that often the old ways are best and a dog can sometimes be better security than technical devices.

This was certainly the opinion of the owner of the car parking facility at Penzance where Theatre Set-Up were obliged to leave their van and car before sailing to the Scilly Isles for performances in St Mary's and Tresco. This dog, a very large German Shepherd dog called Sailor, made sure with his teeth bared and threatening bark that no unauthorised person could enter the enclosed car parking yard or rob any of the vehicles (like Theatre Set-Up's van) parked just outside it. Over the many years that Theatre Set-Up came to Penzance Anne and this dog became friends and every year when the company came to park their vehicles, Sailor's owner would release him, much to the horror of the actors who did not know of his special relationship with Anne, and he would greet her as a long-lost friend. However one evening Anne saw him keeping guard in the parking enclosure and expecting a friendly welcome, approached him as usual. Bared teeth, threatening posture and barking made it quite clear that he was then working, that this was not friendly territory and she would be given the same treatment meted out to anyone straying there.

At Plas Newydd in 1981 Anne could not understand why a dog was keeping constant watch outside one of the outer buildings of the mansion. The custodian, on the other hand, was full of admiration for the dog who, he explained, was courting a bitch there.

"Good on you boy", he called to the dog, "you deserve her". "And at just the right time", he said, "She turns her bum."

There was always a friendly welcome from the house dogs at Pencarrow in Cornwall. In all its printed material Theatre Set-Up always advised its audiences, "Please bring own folding chair or rug". Anne commented to the dog's owner that one of the house dogs must have been able to read one of these signs as when she appeared on site this dog brought her a rug in its mouth as if to show that it was ready, like the Pencarrow visitors, to sit in the audience.

"He's a retriever," explained the dog's owner. "He will always welcome you by bringing something to you in his mouth."

This hospitality, typical of the generosity of the human owners of Pencarrow, became increasingly bizarre as the dog presented Anne with whatever he could find in the house or garden. There were beautiful antique dolls on display in the house and on one occasion the dog appeared with a pair of Victorian doll knickers in its mouth. His presents became even more embarrassingly inappropriate when he appeared at Anne's music desk with expensive exotic plants between his teeth that he had rifled from the garden pond. His owners always forgave him for whatever wrong he had done, as he was a very affectionate dog with what seemed to be a permanent smile on his face.

A large beagle dog with floppy ears called Harold rejoiced at the chance a Theatre Set-Up performance in the Temple Amphitheatre, Chiswick in 2005, gave him to achieve an ambition to jump into its central pond. Evidently he had been taken for his daily walk past the amphitheatre and had looked longingly at the pond, prevented by going into it for an enjoyable swim by the fence which surrounded the site. On this occasion the gate in the fence was open to allow the audience to enter, and taking his chance, Harold escaped from his owner who frantically called out to him as he raced through the gate and bounded down the terraced slopes of the amphitheatre, his ears flapping wildly, at last plunging into the pond and swimming around it in delight. It took some time for his embarrassed owner to persuade him to come out of the pond and to succumb to being put on a lead for an exit through the amused audience settling down to eat their picnics before the play began.

A reference to a dog far from the scene of the performances caused a hiatus in the performance of *Romeo and Juliet* in 1996. The actress performing Juliet, Victoria Stillwell, loved dogs, later abandoning her acting career for one specialising in dog behaviour, presented on television in the UK and the USA under the title of "It's Me or the Dog". Anne was performing her favourite stage role of the Nurse in the play and was waiting offstage for her cue to enter into the play's action when she began to tell Victoria about the games she enjoyed playing with Oscar, the much-loved dog which lived downstairs with her neighbours. Both she and Victoria became so engrossed with this description that Anne missed her cue and was astonished to be hauled by her arm onto the stage by the actor also directing the play that year. Considerable bruising on her arm reminded her of the occasion and her need to prioritise the stage action rather than remembering the beloved Oscar.

Sometimes dogs in the Theatre Set-Up performance sites were an integral part of the house arrangements. Muffin, a tiny dog at Kentwell Hall, Suffolk was one of these. At the site visit during which Anne and the property's owner were deciding on the location of the play, they chose a bank beside the Hall's moat. The plan was that the audience would sit on the opposite bank which slanted down to the moat, providing a tiered effect in rows of chairs one above the other. Muffin seemed to question the wisdom of this as she stood sideways

13

on the audience bank with a quizzical look at her owner. In spite of her disapproval of this arrangement, the performance went ahead in this location, but the back legs of the audience chairs had to be fixed into the bank. This was fine when rain had made the bank soft, but dry hard conditions made this impossible and endorsed Muffin's criticism as the audience tried not to be tipped forward into the moat on their sloping chairs.

The dog with the most site responsibility was Topsy of the Baroniet of Rosendal, Norway. She welcomed in all the hundreds of visitors who came to her resplendent home and was in charge of general security. She became very disturbed during a 1996 rehearsal in the Baroniet courtyard of the duel between the actors performing the characters of Tybalt and Mercutio in *Romeo and Juliet.*

"Fighting in my courtyard?" she seemed to be exclaiming. "Which of these is the guilty cause of it?"

She watched for a short while and then, taking her decision, bounded reprovingly over to the actor playing Tybalt, the belligerent character in the play. Such accurate discrimination complemented not only her ability to detect Tybalt's aggression, but the actor's intention and portrayal of this characteristic of the role.

In Cornwall people were often given permission to bring their dogs to the performances. At one of the performances of *A Midsummer Night's Dream* in 1995 in Trevarno there were 13 dogs of varied species in the audience. The actor performing Puck made a sudden loud entrance onto the stage and all the 13 dogs barked their alarm in a cacophony of tones. It was a good moment in the play, heightening Puck's supposed supernatural presence!

In 2011, much to the amazement of the local animals who had become accustomed to the peace of a semi-wild garden haven, permission was given to the company to rehearse the play in a rear extension of a suburban garden which backed onto a park and would not thus disturb any neighbours. Foremost of these animals was Duke, a huge Great Dane dog whose fenced garden adjoined the rehearsal area. He had made acquaintance with members of the company while taking his master for a walk in the nearby street and had enjoyed their admiring attention. When their rehearsals began he had no intention of allowing that to cease as he thrust his head above the fence of his home waiting for the expected patting of his head to occur. Of course the cast did not want him to feel rejected and the appearance of his head above the fence always created a break in the rehearsal schedule.

The dog who belonged to the owners of the rehearsal space was Otto, a lively dachshund. One of the company's cast members owned the house and garden next door and had always had problems keeping Otto out of his garden into which he could wriggle through gaps in the dividing hedge. You can imagine Otto's indignation when he saw this neighbour delivering his spoken lines and being put through his paces in the play in what Otto considered to be his own territory. He stood looking at the actor in dumbfounded disbelief at the outrageous cheek of it!

Other creatures, accustomed to being able to wander freely through the rehearsal space, watched the unfolding of the play with astonishment. A neighbouring cat took advantage of the roof of a shed at the edge of the garden area to survey the extraordinary proceedings in the style of an attentive member of a theatre audience in the dress circle. This was at an advanced stage in the rehearsal schedule and the cat obviously could not understand the formality of the action, lacking the spontaneity of the human behaviour usually manifest in this spot!

SHEEP

Many of the beautiful sites where Theatre Set-Up's performances were held were surrounded by grazing sheep. These contributed to the pastoral reality of performances of *As You Like It* in Bowhill, Scotland. During any scenes involving the characters of the shepherds in the play the actors offstage used to enjoy making sheep noises. These were so realistic at Bowhill that the sheep in an adjacent field responded loudly and ran towards the tents to recover which of their flock they assumed had strayed there.

FISH

A fish made a surprise appearance at the performance of *A Midsummer Night's Dream* in 1983 at Sudeley Castle. The actor performing Starveling as the *Pyramus and Thisbe* play's character of the moon had a carved flat wooden dog representing the moon which he usually flung away sulkily at the interruption of his performance by the characters playing the courtiers. On this occasion, aware that the wooden dog would float, he flung it into the pond. This startled one of the carp there which leapt into the air in protest, giving the audience a rare performance of the play involving a leaping fish.

HORSES

Horses from another event being presented at Carisbrooke Castle, Isle of Wight, gave one of the performances there considerable problems. Unfortunately the entrance of the company's vehicles clashed with the exit of the horses and the gear they were pulling. The nature of the terrain made it difficult for either side to back off and after the vehicles were driven to one side the horses struggled past. The next day the owners of the horses were so angered by the incident that they piled their rubbish by the theatre company's changing tents, an action which the company, given the strength of the horses, wisely chose to ignore.

A FOX

The actress performing in the 1995 performance of *A Midsummer Night's Dream* wore a long curly red wig for the role of Hippolyta which she put with her costume in the off-stage right changing area of an open air performance of the play at Wollaton Hall, Nottingham. When she came to change into it she was alarmed to see a fox racing off into the distance, the red wig in its mouth. Evidently the fox had mistaken it for one of its cubs. She later complained:

"It is a dreadful thing to see the wig which transforms your character being carted off by a fox!"

A STUFFED GIRAFFE

Wollaton Hall provided the play and its audience with an indoor alternative venue in its hall should the weather be stormy. In the early days of performances there the space where the play could be performed was set out as a museum of stuffed exotic animals. Most of these were in glass cases, glaring with artificial eyes at both the actors and the audiences, but the huge giraffe stood proudly at the back of the audience area with some seating beneath it. Children were especially astonished at the size of its masculine glory when they looked up at it during the performance!

INSECTS

Any outdoor venue is likely to run the gauntlet of insects which plague both members of the audience and the actors. Theatre Set-Up discovered that the insects in Northumberland, Yorkshire and Cornwall were far more robust and numerous than in any other county. Over the years, strategies had to be developed to cope with this. Any exposed flesh of the actors (as well as the tights-clad legs of male actors) always needed to be sprayed with insect-repellent, and mosquito coils were always lit beside the changing tents to the sides of the stage and often interspersed with the sun-floods lighting placed in an arc at the front of the stage area. On one occasion when Anne was commuting between her teaching job in London and performances in the grounds of Wallington Hall, Northumberland, she arrived ready to change into costume and do her stage make-up minutes before the start of the play. She was hit by a wall of insects as she rushed to the changing area.

"Quick, everybody," she shouted to the cast, "Do as I am doing. Put on loads of insect-repellent to see if that will help!"

However such was the density of the insect hoards that even that was insufficient, as the insects went into the open eyes of the actors and into their mouths as soon as they opened them to deliver their lines! When Anne suggested to the gardeners of the venue that the site of the play should be sprayed to kill any insects, they were most offended:

"The insects live here. They were here first. You are only visitors!"

Anne adopted a strategy to help members of the audience in insect-plagued venues. This was necessary not only to protect them from irritation and possible bites from the insects, but to stop them twitching and flicking them away during the performances. This constant movement would be a distraction for both people in the audience and the actors. Therefore before performances guaranteed to be insect-bound, Anne would go around the audience offering to put insect repellent on the hands of anyone who had not provided themselves with their own repellent and then they could apply it themselves to any exposed flesh, plus over their hair, into which insects loved to nestle! This usually worked but sometimes an extra application had to be made in the interval before the second half of the play. Insect repellent became a very essential part of the company's gear!

In the early days of the company's tours the primitive sun-floods which lit the play in an arc around the stage area were not glass-fronted, and insects, attracted to the light-bulbs, would be burnt by them, sending smoke rising as if in their funeral pyres. On one occasion the smell of this smoke alarmed the company's patron during a performance in his garden on Tresco, as his property on the mainland had recently been largely burnt down and he rushed to the scene to see if another fire had also been ignited, this time in his island home.

On the Isle of Wight, sensitive local residents were more concerned about the cruel fate of the insects themselves:

"Please can you get sun-floods with glass on the front to protect the insects. We can't stand seeing them burn to their deaths during the play and cannot come to performances again if this continues."

Fortunately it was possible to replace the old sun-floods with new glass-fronted ones and everyone was happier.

However some actors (like the residents of the Isle of Wight) became upset by any of the operations of the company causing the accidental deaths of insects and they were distressed by the deaths of insects who crashed into the windscreens of the travelling vehicles. It was a company rule that, with the exception of touring to venues many miles apart, the company vehicles should not travel very fast. Thus generally any insects accidentally landing on the windscreens had time to escape from them.

In some areas, however, where many animals were in fields beside the roads on which the company was travelling, there were so many insects in the surrounding air that many met a sad fate on the windscreens. The car carrying three actors always followed the van (a customised white Mercedes Benz high-top van) fairly closely so that the company was travelling in a safe convoy. On one of the occasions when suicidal insects on the windscreen were distressing actors in the car, the actor who was driving the car decided to create a diversion by singing the main songs from "Half a Sixpence," the musical he had recently been performing in. He was an excellent singer and soon all the actors in the car joined in singing with him. Soon this impromptu performance became the main focus of attention in the car and the task of following the company van was neglected. After a while someone in the car noticed that the route the car was following was not the one leading to the venue where the performance would be held that evening.

"Oh, where are we?" the driver cried, "I've been religiously following the company van."

Looking at the white van in front of the car more closely, everyone in the car shouted out:

"You've been following the wrong white van!"

So in future journeys in which many insects performed death crashes onto the car's windscreen, sung diversions were monitored by the car's passengers to ensure that the insects' accidental self-sacrifices were not revenged by their souls causing the car driver to lose sight of the lead vehicle, and steps were taken to ensure that right white van was followed!

CHAPTER 2

"FOR THE RAIN
IT RAINETH EVERY DAY"

RAIN AND INDOOR ALTERNATIVE VENUES

The free-from insect audiences like those in Wollaton Hall who were happily accommodated inside when inclement weather made the outdoor performances challenging, rejoiced in the comfort of the dry conditions so different from those experienced by casts and audiences when no alternative spaces inside were available and performances braved rain, wind and cold.

It is a tradition of English outdoor theatre that should an indoor alternative for the performance not be available and unless the weather produces a dangerous electric storm, the performance continues in any rain that should fall on the performance. Aware of this tradition (which people often elsewhere class as English eccentricity), Anne followed this principle in all the Theatre Set-Up venues when she founded the company, the policy being advertised on all printed material as "Performances continue regardless of weather". Regular members of the theatre seasons' audiences would always come prepared for this, wearing warm, rain-proofed clothing. It would have been inconsiderate to people sitting behind them for audience members to put up umbrellas, so their weather protection had to include rain-proof headgear and covering for all the body including the legs. It was discovered that two black plastic bags served these necessary functions and the company learnt to take rolls of these to give out to unprepared people in the audience. The performances in the Chateau de Prangins, Switzerland, organised by very efficient people from the USA, went one better than this and in rained-on performances provided the audiences with hooded plastic ponchos which they reclaimed at the end of the performance, only the actors becoming drenched.

Sometimes the initial rehearsals for the plays in the "home" London venues were threatened with rain. Technical and dress rehearsals were usually re-scheduled inside any possible available space no matter how small, as the chaos of drying out soaked costumes would have delayed the opening performances. However sometimes during earlier rehearsals if relative shelter beneath trees was not available, the rehearsal had to take place in the rain. This occurred to spectacular effect in 2005 in the garden of The Bothey, Avenue House Grounds, London N3, when Lindsay Royan, the choreographer, needed to teach some of the actors a comic dance that was required for performances of *Love's Labours' Lost*. As this needed to be blocked into the actual stage space, it was not possible to plan them inside the only small room available. Anne and the actors not needed for the dance were then treated to the extraordinary sight of Lindsay and the dancing actors vigorously performing a comic period dance executed with admired accuracy in the driving rain!

The first rained on performance that the company endured was in *As You Like It* in the grounds of Wallington Hall, Northumberland in 1980. The actor playing the character of Charles the Wrestler was bare-chested in the role and as the torrents of rain poured off him, one of the other actors commented that he actually looked as if he were taking a shower, and only the lack of a "soaping" blocked that illusion. Anne moved performances in Wallington to earlier in the season when heavy rain was less likely, but moderate rain often occurred, the stoical Northumbrian audiences ignoring it with full houses of 400 people every night of the five performances there. The actors were astonished when people turned up in wet weather and complained of being turned away when the allowed quota of 400 in the audience had been reached. Each year there was a group of people, who, regardless of the weather, always liked to stay on the performance site of the play after it was over, huddled together by the lighting poles. This was because they wanted to see their delicious picnic desserts as they were eating them. The actors called them "The Strawberry People". Local residents explained to the actors that if Northumbrians did not tolerate events in rain there would be no events at all!

Many people in the audiences went to the performances to enjoy this unconventional form of theatre but most of the actors dreaded the stormed-on performances. They were aware that their shouted dialogue was probably in vain because often audiences, in spite of weather-proofed sound amplification, could not hear the dialogue in the rain from under their headgear. For the actors it was like performing the plays while in the shower and the knowledge that the costumes would need to be dried off before the next performance was galling. Anne always advised the actors anticipating a dreaded rained-on performance with the words:

"It shows that we are prepared to do it!"

The Forty Hall audiences in the venue on the West Lawn which was home to the company from 1976 to 2006, became very astute in wet weather provision. Parents with children would bring small tents for them which they put up at the edges of the auditorium area and the children would watch the play from the tents' doorways. As Forty Hall was open to the public, gangs of unruly youths roamed in it and could have sabotaged the plays' performances there. Anne found that the best way to cope with them was to invite them to come to the performances as guests. Many members of the audience, those not with their children in tents on the edges of the stage area but at the front, joined in this hospitality, sparing the youths from sitting on the damp grass:

"Would you like to sit on our rugs?"

Anne learnt to make sure that the costumes were made of materials which did not become bedraggled when soaked with rain. Silk velvet and brocade were good for this and feathers and net were out! "Wet weather" cloaks, made of rain-repellent materials such as trevira and woollen cloth (but never plastic which would destroy the period look of the costumes) were always set, ready to wear if the weather became wet, in the casts' changing tents. These protected the actors' shoulders and part of the costumes but had to be open to allow for arm gestures. Out of consideration to those who were responsible for drying out the costumes, it was a rule of the company to wear these cloaks when the weather was wet. Wigs with hats sewn onto them generally protected the actors' heads but when the women actors wore veils (always, however made of nylon chiffon which tolerated rain), attached to headbands in Renaissance-styled productions, their hair became soaked. The drying out of the costumes became a stressful necessity after a drenched performance. Anne's garage had been equipped with clothes lines and heaters so a return to London guaranteed their drying out there, often the heritage sites had boiler rooms which could function as drying out areas, and sometimes there were sympathetic land-ladies who could supply a heated room where the costumes could be hung on their costume rails, but if none of these means were available, the dripping garments had to be hung on their rails in Anne's bedroom in the digs at the risk of her health!

There were a number of locations which were guaranteed to produce deluging rain. These were mostly located in Cornwall, Northumberland and the Isle of Man. The performance in 1984 of *Love's Labour's Lost* in Trelissick Gardens, Cornwall, was rained on so thoroughly that a picture of one of its drenched scenes was put on the front page of The Western Morning News under the headline, "Love's Labours' Drowned". The costumes were so wet that they had to be taken to a local sympathetic laundry to be dried out. It rained so often on the performance site at Cotehele, Cornwall, that on one occasion when the weather was dry Anne lost her way to the venue as it seemed so unfamiliar.

The Scillonian venues of the gardens in The Chaplaincy on the island of St Mary's and Tresco Abbey were exposed to the sudden downpours which could sweep in from the Atlantic Ocean. One of these surprised the performance of *Much Ado About Nothing* in the Tresco Abbey gardens in 1981. The actor performing the role of Leonato, Hero's father, always insisted on spraying his hair silver in order to convey a greater age of the character than his own 30-odd years. As the rain poured down on him, this silver ran down his face giving the impression that he was playing the "tin man" from the *Wizard of Oz*. Many members of the audience who had come to Tresco in their tiny boats from neighbouring islands came backstage to tell Anne how much, in spite of the rain, and perhaps, due to the fun of incidents like the silvered face of Leonato, they had enjoyed the performance:

"We may die trying to get home, but we will die happy!"

The performances of the plays in the gardens of Mount Edgecumbe, Cornwall, were held on a series of steps framing a small terrace and surmounted by statues. During a typically Cornish downpour of rain on a performance in 1987 of *The Two Gentlemen of Verona*, these steps became water cascades and the management of the site, recognising the danger to the actors who were finding it difficult to stand or walk in these torrents, stopped the performance and kindly transferred it into their long restaurant. Everyone was very pleased and in future years if rain was forecast or if it occurred during the performance, the restaurant became the venue for the performances of the plays.

In subsequent years, with the exception of Trevarno where it only rained once on performances, Cornish venues were chosen which had indoor alternatives, usually in the sites' restaurants. Sometimes the kindness of the administrators or owners of venues made luxurious alternative rooms to become available for otherwise stormed on performances. In 2011 there was advance warning of the storm about to hit the performance of *Much Ado About Nothing* in Pencarrow so there were very few audience members brave enough to turn up. Seeing this, the owners allowed the performance to take place in the majestic library room of the house where the audience and the play could be comfortably accommodated. The result was one of the most beautiful Theatre Set-Up performances ever presented as the period costumes chimed with the period of the room. Powderham Castle, over the border in Devon, allowed their beautiful music room to be used as an alternative venue to the stormy outside for a performance of *The Merry Wives of Windsor* in 1985 with a similar magnificent result.

The audience numbers for the company's performances held in Fountains Abbey in Yorkshire were always guaranteed to be high as people knew that if rain fell on the outdoor location in Fountain Abbey's huge courtyard, the play would be accommodated in the abbey's large Cellarium where the Abbey's past monk inhabitants had stored the vast quantities of the grain that they had grown in their fields as well as their renowned kegs of monastery-brewed beer. This transfer to a dry location could even be done within reason during a possible break in the play's action during the performance if the heavens opened. This occurred one year when the play and its audience moved into the Cellarium during a convenient break in the play's action when a downpour threatened to soak the event. The stage manager set up the play across the centre of this long, wide medieval cellar with a view on one side open to the sky through its pillars, with the audience comfortably facing the stage action from either side. Very soon everyone settled down, the electrics were fixed so that the harp music could be amplified and several sun-floods could provide an additional glow to the evening's pale light, props and costume changes were set in nearby alcoves of this new location and the actors prepared to re-start the play. It so happened that this rain was only a passing shower, but the audience generally did not mind that they were tucked up inside the building while clear skies revealed themselves over the previous outdoor location of the play. However one gentleman, considerably worse for wear from his overindulgence in the red wine whose near-empty bottle he was clutching in his hand, tottered to his feet and proclaimed loudly in a crisp southern English accent:

"The rain has stopped now. Can I respectfully ask the organisers of the play to transfer us outside again."

This did not go down well with the pragmatic Yorkshire audience, by then comfortably seated on their folding chairs and beginning to eat their picnics which they had laid out before them.

"Sit down and be quiet," shouted a man from the back of the audience, "We're from Yorkshire!"

Sadly lacking the comfort of an indoor alternative like that of Fountains Abbey, the Isle of Man's Peel Castle venue was open to the elements at all times. The rain there had the added factor of strong winds, making it horizontal. Ironically, Theatre Set-Up's first experience of this was on the last night of their initial performances of *The Tempest* there in 1982. Anne had set up a challenge to the Manx audiences during an interview on Manx radio:

"If it rains on our performances on the Isles of Scilly or the Isle of Wight the audience stays put. Do you get the point, Isle of Man?"

Responding to this challenge during the horizontal rain pouring down on the last night's performances, the members of the audience, well protected by oilskin rainwear, sat calmly passing chocolate cake to each other and drinking wine from silver goblets. That showed Anne how stoical they were in comparison to other island audiences! This hardened Anne's attitude to the actors:

"You look cold. Put on a brighter lipstick!" she hissed at the shivering actresses.

The cast were always happy to know that any wet weather threatening performances of the plays in The Lost Gardens of Heligan, Cornwall, could be disregarded as the plays could be transferred completely into the restaurant, large enough to take the performance of the play and a sizable audience. In 2006 the performance of *The Winter's Tale* unusually had some set (a construction which served as the revealing space for the seeming statue of the very alive Hermione in Act V) which needed to be transferred into the indoor location. The stage manager organised all the cast to carry this large object (which had already been set up before the rain set in) into the restaurant. Members of the audience cheered as the set was plonked down safely by all the cast, who then took a bow.

Some venues had alternative indoor venues booked beforehand in case of rain. This happened in Jersey in 1996 for a performance of *The Comedy of Errors* on a night when a storm was forecast. The local theatre was then advertised as the location of the play usually presented during that week in the Middle Ward of Mont Orgeuil Castle. Anne had experienced an unusual interview with a local radio reporter there. He wanted to get the sound of the sea as a backdrop to his interview and for this he took Anne to a park by the sea, where she was stood up against a tree. Unfortunately dozens of ants decided that she must be a branch of this tree and began to run up her legs, quickly terminating the interview. The spectacular Mont Orgeuil had provided not only a magnificent backdrop for the play but astonished audiences on one night when its reflection was imprinted as a shadow on a large cloud to the leeward of the castle. This phenomenon effectively upstaged any stage action! A completely different kind of performance had to be rehearsed when the play was scheduled to be performed inside a regular theatre in St Helier on the stormy night and a stage lighting plan evolved. The cast, accustomed to indoor theatre performances with other companies, were delighted at the prospect of performing the play on the stage of a purpose-built theatre with comfortable dressing rooms, accessible toilets and no problems with trying to be heard above rough winds and driving rain!

This delight was repeated when Anne decided to present the play each year for one night in Millfield Theatre, North London, as an indoor alternative to the outdoor Forty Hall performances for the benefit of regular audience members now too old or fragile to face the chilly weather of the West Lawn. This decision meant that some kind of collapsible set had to be designed, then conveniently available for all the alternative indoor venues, always transported in the top box or boot of Anne's car. Material components were the most successful of these, often painted banners. Good examples of these fabric "sets" were the Indian saris, stretched out from a central point upstage which provided very adequate staging for *Antony and Cleopatra* in 1989. The audiences accommodated in the alternative indoor venues were very pleased with these instant sets which turned any space into a theatre. If the space did not have overhead bars from which to hang banners or other set items, the stage manager used the lighting poles which were always carried in the van. These "sets" sometimes comprised Anne's curtains from Kashmir, but usually they were banners attached to garden canes or narrow wooden poles which could be rolled up together and fit into a small bag. These were designed and painted by our "props/hats/ shoes/mask" designer, Andrew Fisher, whose ingenuity was always appreciated by casts and audiences.

This instant portable form of theatre set was regarded as unusual by some of the European theatres in which Theatre Set-Up performed. When, in 1994 Theatre Set-Up presented performances of *The Taming of the Shrew* in Das SchlossTheater im Neuen Palais im Park, Sanssouci, Potsdam, Germany (built for Frederick the Great of Prussia), the administrators of the theatre, accustomed to sets made of stage flats of painted canvas and wood asked Anne during the site visit:

"Where is your set?"

"In my handbag," she replied, bringing out her four Kashmir-embroidered 15 foot long curtains and several lengths of string with which to gather them up into artistic drapes. Observing the gilded sculpted hanging grapes decorating the images of musical instruments and tall young men in the decor of the theatre, Anne decided to try to find plastic grapes which she would spray gold to match the theatre's décor to tie into the points of the curtains where they were gathered up. Potsdam's florist shops were then denuded by Anne of their plastic grapes which, gilded and placed strategically on the gathered curtains, made the set ready. Everyone was delighted with this set, a direct descendent of the indoor alternative sets designed for avoiding rained on performances in the UK. The stage manager of the Sanssoucci theatre was especially pleased with the effectiveness of this "curtain set" as were the actors, happily dry amid the familiar drapes inside this historic building.

Rothley Court, Leicester, where the plays were presented in the beautiful gardens of the grounds, was able to supply an indoor rained on weather alternative in the Templars' place of worship, also in the grounds. Anne and the actors had not realised that the Templars were still active and were delighted to see a future for the organisation in the notices in the building of a Templar Sunday School for the children. Fortunately there was a raised area in the building where the play could be performed with the audience seated on church pews. Cast and audience alike appreciated the generosity of the Templars which spared them getting wet in providing this refuge from the rain!

Often children loved rained-on performances, the sense of adventure enhancing their experience of the play. Venues in Yorkshire were often rained on and at a performance in Harlow Carr Botanical Gardens, Harrogate of *A Midsummer Night's Dream* in 2000 the young school children sitting at the front of the audience area were squealing with delight as they emerged for the interval from under their tarpaulin rain-cover:

"Isn't this wonderful!" they shrieked to Anne as she shivered with her harp beneath the large music umbrella.

Some members of the Yorkshire audiences decided that the indoor venue in Harrogate of the Sun Pavilion, Valley Gardens, would provide an escape for the performances from the inevitable Yorkshire damp and midges. Theatre Set-Up took up this suggestion and performed there in subsequent years. Some members of the audience were grumpy at this transfer inside as they were unable to munch away during the performance at the picnics that they had always enjoyed at the outside locations. However during the first performance of the company in the Sun Pavilion, the heavens opened during the second half of the play, pelting rain on the stained glass Victorian domed roof:

"Aren't you glad you're inside?" Anne shouted loudly above the noise of the rain on the dome from her now appreciably-dry music desk.

Often Anne's harp seemed to resonate more fully from under the music umbrella during rained on performances than it did during dry evenings. This occurred to a significant extent in a performance of *A Midsummer Night's Dream* in 1983 in the moat-surrounded island of Scotney Castle. Both actors and audience were getting soaked, but the harp, when played, was singing its heart out from under its shelter. The agent of one of the actors was regretting that he had come to see his client perform in this performance as his rainwear had not kept him dry in the deluge:

"You and the harp were evidently all right under your umbrella!" he shouted resentfully to Anne as he sloshed his way up the steep path to the car park after the performance.

There was cover provided for the audience in the venue in Cossington Manor Gardens, Somerset, but the stage area lay open to the sky. This produced heavy rain in a performance of *Cymbeline* in 2009. It was one of those occasions when the audience appreciated the play not only for its performance but for the stoicism of the actors. In particular one of the actors had been born and brought up on the Isle of Man, so he was in his element in driving rain, and his enthusiasm as he splashed his way across the stage in this watery medium so familiar to him amazed the audience and encouraged the other actors to endure their way to the end of the play's Act V. It was one of the venues where superb hospitality was given and the soaked cast were warmed by an excellent hot meal provided by the hosts of Cossington Manor at the end of the evening.

In 2008 the Anglican church was provided as a refuge from a forecast storm in the Scillonian island of St Mary's. The plays were usually performed in the garden terraces of the church's Chaplaincy sub-tropical gardens and had often carried on in slight drizzle, but the forecast Atlantic storm would have been dangerous to the audience and cast. In consideration of the facts of this church-rescue, Anne was somewhat peeved when some members of the audience complained of the distorted acoustics of the play in the changed location!

ELECTRICAL STORMS

It was dangerous to perform in any electrical storms that should descend on any of the outdoor venues and one of these occurred near the end of a matinee performance for schools in 1983 of *A Midsummer Night's Dream* in the Rookery, Streatham Common, London. With thunder and lightning preceding heavy rain, the danger to the actors who were performing beneath a tree capable of being a lightning con-ductor was imminent. From beneath the umbrella sheltering her (as the play's musician), her small harp and Celtic drum, Anne shouted out to the audience of school children (whose reckless teachers were trying to persuade them to be stoical and stay put,) and to the actors:

"Run for your lives!"

They did so and as he passed, the actor performing the *Pyramus and Thisbe* role of the "Wall" in the play from beneath a huge box which served to represent the wall, took the harp from under Anne's umbrella, and protecting it from the rain under his box-wall carried it to safety in the gardeners' shed. Anne was in considerable danger from any electricity from the lightning which might be conducted down the metal pole of the umbrella, so she wrapped the Celtic drum in her cloak and ran with it to the nearest shelter beneath a section of the garden. With insufficient protection from her cloak for the drum which would have been ruined by getting wet had she proceeded further, she was marooned there for the following two hours until the storm ceased. Her return then to the gardeners' shed was greeted by surprised cries from the actors who by then had presumed that she had been struck dead by lightning beneath her umbrella!

The only considered mishap caused by that storm was the supposed loss of the small bell which Anne or the stage manager would ring vigorously to signal the end of the play's interval so that the audience would know to return to their places in the "auditorium" for the continuance of the play. However six months later it arrived in a parcel sent by the Rookery gardeners to Anne's flat. It had been buried by the power of the rain in the part of the garden where Anne's umbrella had been during the storm and had gradually made its way up to the surface in the following months. Whenever it was rung in future performances, whoever was ringing the bell always pointed out to the audiences its celebrity status:

"This is the bell which was buried by a storm and immolated for six months in the gardens of the Rookery, Streatham Common."

In 1985 the cast of *The Merry Wives of Windsor* were looking forward to their performance at Blickling Hall, Norfolk. The Times newspaper, noting the Hall as the ancient home of Sir John Fastolfe, the supposed origin of the play's character, Sir John Falstaff, had taken a photo of several Theatre Set-Up actors performing characters in the play against the backdrop of the Hall and put it on page three of their morning paper. This should have pleased the National Trust who owned the property as it might have attracted a large audience to the play's performance. However a severe storm was forecast for the evening and as the performance was scheduled to be held in the open air, bookings for the performance were few. The cast had gone ahead to Blickling Hall and had already set up the lighting, changing areas etc outside, while Anne, who had been teaching during the day, followed on later. As she drove to Norfolk, the storm, which had taken on the physical nature of a cyclone, hit the road upon which Anne was travelling. Many cars wisely stopped by the side of the road to let the storm pass, some of them brought to a halt by the pelting rain which had flooded their engines. Anne's car, being fairly high, was able to keep going and she accelerated to a pace which took her through the still centre of the "cyclone" and out the other side through its pelting rain. She just beat the storm to Blickling Hall, rushed to where the actors were setting up the play and yelled:

"Quick, take everything down and put it inside the van or the building."

One of the actors said later that he had never seen her face as white or terrified as at that moment. The actors quickly took everything down, putting it either in the van or inside a room in the Hall before the storm struck with a fury that would have destroyed all the gear and possibly injured the actors. The National Trust found an inside space within which the play and its tiny audience could be accommodated and the performance went ahead there. Sadly no future performances were ever scheduled for the company at Blickling Hall as in spite of the prestigious Times coverage (worth £17,000 at the time), the National Trust complained of their loss of revenue that evening! Anne was just glad that she had been delayed from arrival at the Hall with the cast, that she had encountered the storm on her journey there and had been able to save the gear and the actors!

However another stormed-on performance which Anne was not able to salvage was the performance in 2002 of *As You Like It* at Broadlands, Hampshire. Apart from the beer tent, set up for refreshments for the audience, there was no alternative indoor space for the performance of the play which continued from its beginning to end in driving rain. Several of the actors questioned why the play was being performed in such adverse conditions but the audience was quorate (higher in number than the number of cast), and therefore the "play must go on". Also the parents of a lead actor were in the audience, ignoring the rain and enjoying seeing their son perform. A diversion from the play occurred when the van carrying the remaining unsold beer was driven through the back of the stage area, making Anne realise that she should have asked permission to hold the performance in the beer tent, thus preventing this distraction from the play and keeping everyone dry!

Aware of the certainty of storms and persistent rain always prevalent in Western Norway, the managers of the Baroniet of Rosendal, Norway, decided that they would cover the courtyard where they had decided they would present the Theatre Set-Up plays with a large plastic sheet, attached at its sides and front to the courtyard walls. In 1993 during the company's performance of *Hamlet* the heavens opened with torrential rain and soon the plastic sheet became filled with water. Seeing that this pool of rain was becoming so enormous that it was weighing down the plastic sheet to the extent that it would soon burst it and inundate all of the audience, the managers of the Baroniet rushed forward, stopped the performance and tried to disperse the water to the back of the plastic sheeting with poles. Soon the water sloshed its way back there and descended in torrents onto the audience sitting at the back of the courtyard. The tolerant members of the Norwegian audience who were sitting at the back of the courtyard, accustomed as they were to being drenched, took this all in good humour but different arrangements had to be made for future years.

When Anne first took the theatre company to the Baroniet, the programme of events arranged for them exceeded their physical capabilities, leaving them exhausted, unlike the Norwegians whose tough Viking ancestry seemed to prevail in their extraordinary ability to endure long hours of strenuous activity. Anne had to alert the managers of the Baroniet to the fact that the Viking ancestry of English people remains too distant in their DNA to match that of the Norwegians and the events schedules would need to be downgraded. This Norwegian Viking physical prowess became a kind of joke between Anne and her Norwegian hosts, animated in their solution in the next year to the flooding of the plastic sheeting over the court-yard. They placed tubes on the plastic cover which could somehow drain the rain from the front to the back of the sheeting. Positioned at the back, each holding one of these tubes were strapping "Viking" girls, sucking in the air at the end of the tubes to create a vacuum which would draw the water to them which they then would pour into a drain at the back of the auditorium. It was extraordinary! Equally extraordinary was the kindness, hospitality and appreciation that the Baroniet's hosts gave the company, providing accommo-dation, meals, banquets after the show and plaudits bestowed with presents and flowers. The extent of this generosity matched the vigour of the "Viking" girls' ability to drain off rain from the plastic cover over the courtyard by sucking air from tubes!

WHEN THE LIGHTING SUDDENLY GOES OUT

Escaping from the often wet presentation of the plays in Scotney Castle, from 1992 onwards performances of Theatre Set-Up in Kent were held inside the beautiful Barons' Hall in Penshurst Place. Not only did this ensure that the audiences and performances could enjoy the shelter of the inside venue (especially as it was always held on the last night of the season so that actors, costumes and all the stage gear could be taken home dry), but the occasions were blessed with a sense of the 15th century antiquity of the Hall, appropriate to the era of the plays and incidentally to the history of the UK. Shakespeare's contemporary, Sir Philip Sidney, had eaten his meals from the long tables by the walls at the side of the audience, and portraits in the house of the family members who had owned Penshurst Place in the past resonated with their function in the annals of the UK. The owners kindly allowed the actors to use the room behind the stage area for their stage right costume changing, entrances and exits. This wonderful room had been set out with written material and display cases enclosing historical items significant to the family and to the country. These exhibits sometimes showed the relationship between members of the family owning Penshurst Place to the monarch of the time. One displayed letter is from the courtier Lady Mary Sidney to people in her home at Penshurst, requesting that they urgently find and send twelve yards of silk for a dress for Queen Elizabeth I of the same material as in a dress she herself had been wearing and which the Queen envied.

(Anne already knew the sad story of Lady Mary Sidney who caught smallpox from Queen Elizabeth I and was so badly scarred that she had to retire from court and live out the rest of her life with her six children immured in Penshurst Place). A more recent item displayed in the room was part of the correspondence file of the family member who had ordered the evacuation of the Allied Army from Dunkirk. This historic letter was from King George VI (in his own handwriting), to Sir Winston Churchill asking him not to take part in person in the D-Day invasion of France in World War II but to remain in London. Anne felt very privileged to be in the presence of such memorabilia in the company's inside refuge from the Kentish autumnal weather.

The owners of Penshurst Place had very wisely never over-painted the walls of the Barons' Hall, dating from the 15th century. The Theatre Set-Up's 1996 production of *Romeo and Juliet* was costumed in period dress of that century, and perfectly matched its setting in the Hall. Regular Theatre Set-Up audience members from Kent who sometimes regretted the outside performances in Scotney Castle were consoled by such occasions in Penshurst Place. One year the stage manager overloaded the circuit of the lighting control equipment and not only were all the lights in the Barons' Hall taken out but those in the residential quarters of Penshurst Place. This attracted the attention of members of the household who very kindly produced a number of candles and proceeded to attach them to the historic candle holders around the Barons' Hall so that the performance could continue until the short circuit could be fixed. The result was a magical setting for the play with the candlelight flickering on the ancient walls, giving the performance a historical perspective.

There was a more dramatic result when a short circuit occurred during a performance of *Much* Ado *About Nothing* in the Ventnor

Botanic Garden on the Isle of Wight in 1999. The local council had decided that they would take the responsibility of lighting the long uphill path along which the members of the audience would exit after the performance. Anne warned them to be careful not to put up lighting which used too much electricity as the company did not want to overload the system. However they took no notice and put strings of electric light bulbs all along the path. This was fine until Theatre Set-Up's own stage lighting was switched on when it became dark at 9pm. Suddenly all the lights went out not only in the Ventnor Botanic Garden but in the whole surrounding area of Ventnor.

The company had trained their loyal audiences at Ventnor to cope with whatever happened, rain, wind or lighting failure, so they sat quietly trying to see the actors who carried on regardless, hoping that someone would fix the problem. After a while during all this fumbling around in the gathering gloom a little boy (much like the one noticing the absence of the emperor's clothes in the famous legend), said in a loud shrill voice to his mother:

"Mummy, we can't see. The lights have gone out!"

"Ssh..." said his mother, "We know. Just be quiet and **listen** to the play."

Theatre Set-Up always had an emergency battery-operated lighting pack available to light them through the end of the packing up of the gear after all their lighting and cables had been put away in the van. Anne knew that the stage manager who would normally deal with technical issues was at the time elsewhere on stage and unable to operate this lighting pack (which had been set stage right at the front of the stage to cope with an emergency like this), so as soon as she had made her exit from the stage she went to this pack and tried to find its switch, turn it on and then focus its lights on the stage action. She was performing the role of the friar in the play and dressed in the appropriate hooded costume. At the same time as she arrived at the lighting pack the Ventnor Botanic Garden custodian who was looking after the production also arrived there, accidentally throwing the light from her torch into Anne's face. Unaware of Anne's role as the friar, she was taken by so much surprise at the sight of this hooded being who looked in the wavering lighting like some monster out of "Star Wars", that she screamed loudly. This stunned Anne so much that she accidentally threw the switch of the lighting pack, rendering it inoperable until it could be charged up again at an electric source. Thus there was no longer any available lighting for the continuation of the play, the custodian supplying the only available illumination from her flickering torch! There was much flickering from torches and candles in that area of Ventnor that night until the electrical system could be fixed.

WIND

Sometimes it was just strong winds which challenged performances of the plays. The Isle of Man specialised in these and played havoc with costumes. Anne had learnt to have the bottom hems of flimsy women's gowns held down with sewn-in metal weights, but this could not be done to any of the head veils. In a performance of *Love's Labours' Lost* in 2005 the veils on the hats of the actresses were blown upright by the strength of the wind for all of the performance. This effect, although comic was at least modest, unlike the result of the wind's caprice with the men's Roman-style tunics in the 2007 performance of *The Comedy of Errors*:

"You have seen more than you have paid for!" Anne protested to the delighted members of the audience as they left after the performance.

The strength of the wind in the performance at Bowhill in Scotland of *All's Well that Ends Well* in 2008 exceeded even the Isle of Man gales. Such was its force that it was almost impossible to put up the changing tents to the right and left of the stage area and certainly impossible to put up the music desk umbrella. Anne was accompanying the play with music on the lute which was almost blown out of her hands throughout the performance. The actors fought to stay upright on stage and made their entrances looking like alpinists trying to ascend Mount Everest. The audience, wrapped warmly in their resplendent tartan rugs and happily eating their picnics, unsympathetically enjoyed the bizarre scene.

COLD

Most of the dry, calm performances held outdoors during the summer evenings were blessed by balmy temperatures until the sun set, after which cold air descended onto audiences and actors alike. As regular members of the audience always brought warm clothing against the chilly late evenings, they were fine. Anne had provided the actors with thermal underwear which would protect them from the cold and any actresses wearing flimsy gowns had warming capes which they could wear if they felt cold, but members of the audience, unused to the chilly evenings and dressed only in the summer clothes appropriate to the earlier part of the day, suffered. Students attending the performance in 1993 of *Hamlet* in The Fountain Garden, Westmere, in the grounds of Birmingham University found the solution to this. After the performance had finished and when the cast were preparing to pack everything into the van, they were astonished to find that the tarpaulin which had covered the gear on the top of the van had been removed. Evidently the students, marshalling their ingenuity in the need to find cover against the cold, had climbed on to the top of the van, removed the tarpaulin and sheltered beneath it at the back of the auditorium area for the cold duration of the performance. Fortunately the actors found the tarpaulin abandoned and hidden behind bushes in the garden when they desperately looked for it to protect the gear packed onto the top of the van.

The performances in Pendennis Castle, Cornwall, usually escaped being rained on but the exposed position on the top of a headland brought exceptional cold. Audiences were prepared to put up with this in order to enjoy the magnificent setting of this castle, built as a fortress on the command of Henry VIII. The performance of *Hamlet* in 1993 was particularly spectacular there, Hamlet's father's ghost haunting the play from the walls of the ramparts. Regular members of the audience and local people aware of the castle's cold and windy location, were comfortably warm as they watched the play from inside their sleeping bags sensibly brought for the purpose. There was a youth hostel beside the castle and its guests, already equipped with their own sleeping bags they needed in the Spartan dormitories of the hostel, often came to the plays. On one occasion a couple from Heidelberg, Germany, rushed to speak to Anne as the play was being set up on the green sward in front of the castle. Wishing to experience the renowned eccentricity of an English outdoor performance, they asked her:

"Please can we get tickets and can we bring our two children?"

"Certainly, but bring your sleeping bags," replied Anne. They did so, enjoyed the play enormously from inside their sleeping bags and became friends with Anne, assisting the performances of the company when they were presented in Heidelberg Castle, Germany in subsequent years. However, due to the wisdom of German audiences who did not enjoy being rained on, or frozen by sharp winds, the performances in this Schloss were held comfortably inside the castle, in the theatre-sized "King's Room", the "Konigsaal". **All the mainland European venues preferred the company's plays to be performed comfortably inside their properties!**

HOT SUN

In matinee performances sometimes it was the hot sun from which some members of the audience tried to escape. The venue held within the embracing circle of a well-established hedgerow tree in the Oakhill Park Arena, in North London, always seemed to have very hot weather during its matinees. Some people, sitting in their comfortable folding or deck chairs, simply lathered themselves with suntan cream and basked in the warmth of the afternoon, watching the play from the designated audience "chair areas". Others lounging on the grass in the "rug areas" in front of them, simply lay down on the grass soaking up the sun with oiled bared flesh.

However many sun-shy people escaped to the shade of the hedgerow tree which was some distance from the stage area, expecting the location of the play to be changed to accommodate them. All that Theatre Set-Up could do to reconcile these different elements of the audience was to perform to the sun-lovers in front of them and set up speakers of their sound system by the hedgerow tree to amplify the plays' dialogue!

CHAPTER 3

"THE ACTORS ARE AT HAND"

HERITAGE VENUES

The audience arrangement which prevailed in most of the Theatre Set-Up UK outdoor venues, where people who had brought their own rugs sat in a designated area at the front of the audience area and those with their chairs sat in orderly rows behind them, was first implemented by the person in charge of two performances of a Celtic-style *The Tempest* given by Theatre Set-Up in 1982 in Stonehenge, (administered at that time by the D.O.E., the Department Of the Environment). The intention had been to mount some performances within the Avebury Stone Circle, but the members of the local parish, objecting to the D.O.E. giving permission for performances to be presented there while they had been refused permission to hold their tea parties by the Stones, created such a fuss that the D.O.E. offered Theatre Set-Up Stonehenge as an alternative venue. Anne jumped at the opportunity this gave for publicity of the event. She telephoned all the national UK papers, the radio and TV stations and said to them:

"I don't know if you are interested in what I have to say, but I am speaking on behalf of the first theatre company in nearly 5,000 years to be given permission to put on performances of a Shakespearean play in Stonehenge."

This ploy was successful and as well as local papers, the national *The Times* and *The Guardian* newspapers sent reporters and photographers to a press conference in Stonehenge which the company was able to hold a week before the performances to be held there, while on their way to venues in Cornwall. National radio and Southern Television also recorded and filmed articles of costumed interviews with Anne and several actors at this press conference. The politically-correct *The Guardian* Newspaper was particularly impressed by the standard of the costumes which the company had made themselves, especially the masks which had been created by the art lecturer in the college where Anne worked (an artist later to be employed by television companies) in the light of the obvious material poverty of the company, evidenced by the ancient company Ford minibus.

"Do you have any Art Council grants?" *The Guardian* press reporter asked Anne.

"No, we do not comply with their stipulated requirement that we should be producing modern plays."

"Outrageous! We will give you everything to help – repeated photos up to and after the performances on major pages of the paper as well as glowing reports!"

The photographer for the Picture Desk section of the national *The Times* newspaper was also impressed by the material standards of the company, matched attractively to the heritage site which provided the setting for the plays. He not only put excellent photos of the Stonehenge *The Tempest* production into its publications that week, but followed up by doing the same in subsequent years. Anne would contact him with the details of one of the heritage venues whose history was reflected in the costumes in that year's schedule of performances. On an agreed date he would take a photograph of several actors in those costumes against the backdrop of the venue at 11 am and the Picture Desk would feature them in *The Times* newspaper that evening. This gave the company a national identity and reputation. So Theatre Set-Up was very grateful for the fuss made by the Avebury parishioners that denied them Avebury but gave them Stonehenge!

The insurance policies needed for public performances of the plays in all the sites had to include one for Public Liability. A phone call had to be made to the insurers concerning the details of the site and its possible risks to the public. Among the questions asked in this interview were:

"What is the age of the property?" and "What is the nature of any features of the property?"

Anne had great fun with the phone call she made concerning the Department Of the Environment properties Theatre Set-Up was performing in the year of the performances in Stonehenge. For the Chiswick Temple Amphitheatre the answers were:

"About five hundred years. Lake surrounded by grassed terraces and a small temple."

For Carisbrooke Castle, Isle of Wight: "About eight hundred years. Large castle."

For Stonehenge: "About five thousand years. Big stones."

The publicity given to the performances in Stonehenge attracted very large audiences which also boosted the company's finances. During the first night of performances there a storm raged, brilliant lightning flashing off the Stones, thunder almost drowning the voices of the actors and the rain soaking the costumes. The next day Anne and the actress performing the role of Miranda spent the day drying out and ironing the costumes so that they appeared refreshed for the second performance which luckily had balmy weather and a full moon hanging behind the henge. It was a remarkable occasion, the beauty and ancient heritage of the setting giving the performance an added magical atmosphere.

Often the magical heritage venues in which the company performed gave the actors a sense of brushing shoulders with Shakespeare himself, or at least with members of his company, The King's Men. This certainly occurred in Heidelberg Schloss. Anne had found readings of alchemy in Shakespeare's plays and had learnt that the castle had a special place in alchemy in his era, especially when Elizabeth, the daughter of King James I who was the patron of Shakespeare's company, The King's Men, married Frederick of Bohemia and lived in the castle. When Anne made her site visit to the castle in the year before the scheduled performance there she announced to the manager of the castle:

"Of course Shakespeare had a special relationship with this castle."

"Yes he did and his company certainly performed in a specially constructed theatre here. However it is not known if Shakespeare was with them at the time. Sadly Napoleon's troupes demolished the building containing the theatre, but if you come through here we will show you the ruins."

Anne was led through a door into the ruins, due to security risks not usually open to the public, and told that Elizabeth and Frederick had built a seven-story tower there, surmounted by a theatre imitating in dimensions and style The Globe theatre in London belonging to The King's Men. It was an amazing incident and gave Anne an imagined sense of the presence of Shakespeare or at least of his fellow actors.

However the memory of his assured presence was evoked in the Great Garden of his Stratford-upon-Avon home, New Place (long since demolished and replaced by another house, so it is now called

Nash's house and New Place). Here Theatre Set-Up performed on the lawn beneath a large mulberry tree, which, due to the colour transition from its white blossoms to the red-purple of its fruit, was thus made significant to alchemy (which was symbolised by a similar symbolic colour change). Unfortunately the tree had already shed its fruit the first time they played there in 2005 with a production of *The Merry Wives of Windsor*. The preparation for the performance included the difficult task of removing all the fruit which lay on the lawn beneath the tree in case its juice stained the costumes. Such was the abundance of the fruit of the tree, indicating a particularly fertile nature of the soil in which it was growing, that Anne was convinced that many people had willed their ashes to be secretly buried there! She learnt to schedule any performances there at a time of year well before its fruit had ripened and fallen on the lawn. This done, the performances had a special quality with the certainty that their author had certainly spent time there during his lifetime, and perhaps the soil in which the tree was growing contained the remains of devotees of his work!

Another site upon which past performances of Shakespeare's company had been performed was the Grand Square of The Royal Naval College, Greenwich. A royal palace, in which both Queen Elizabeth I and James I had hosted performances of Shakespeare's company and which had long-since been demolished, had been there in his era. Anne announced this fact to the resident chaplain of the Royal Naval College who had invited her to tea there with his family one autumn evening.

Looking out of a window at the magnificence of the buildings surrounding the Square, the chaplain commented:

"You are looking at one of the creations of Sir Christopher Wren."

"That is not all that I am looking at," responded Anne. "I am seeing the site where a royal palace once stood and where Shakespeare and his fellow actors are recorded as having performed many times."

"Then we must arrange performances of your company to be put on there in remembrance of that significant fact!"

It was thus that Theatre Set-Up performed in the Grand Square for several years. When negotiating the details of the projected performances with the administration of the Royal Naval College, Anne was surprised to discover that it was regarded in all senses as a ship of the Royal Navy. This presented a problem in 1987 when the company was informed that during the performance of *The Two Gentlemen of Verona* another Royal Navy ship would be passing along the Thames and the required salute between the "vessels" would take place. However the actors were up to the task. When the salute began to take place the actress performing Silvia who was then centre stage in the performance, turned towards the Thames, saluted the passing ship, and indicating that all the audience and cast should stand and follow suit, she announced:

"Behold, my father's ship!"

Sadly the actors' happy accommodation of Royal Navy events broke down in the following year when a conflict of interests between the performance of the play and a social event of the Royal Naval College took place. The driver of a bus carrying personnel from the Royal Navy insisted on driving his bus through the audience area and disrupting the performance in order to reach his destination in the college buildings. It effectively destroyed the sense which had been built up in previous years of the history of Shakespeare's presence on that site and future performances were cancelled.

This sense of Shakespeare's past presence had also occurred in 1982 when Theatre Set-Up was asked to put on a performance in the building which had been constructed over the newly-discovered remains in the building's basement of the Elizabethan theatre, the Rose, in which Shakespeare had performed in the early years of his career. There was considerable national and international publicity over the discovery of this iconic site and theatre celebrities staged protests that it should be conserved and permanently displayed to the public. However because the visible ruined parts of this theatre were subject to decay if exposed and needed to be immediately re-buried, not only was this not practicable but no performance was possible in the actual theatre itself. Instead Anne was asked to present their performance of *The Merchant of Venice* in a large area of the office block above it. The Theatre Set-Up charitable directors and the owners of the building all contributed to creating in the office area a stage with the exact measurements of its counterpart in the basement, enclosed by Anne's Kashmir–embroidered curtains and surrounded by dozens of artificial roses (chosen to reflect the original theatre's name) and artificial bushes so that the office looked like a garden with the theatre at its heart. It was a private performance given by the office block's owners to The National Trust of England as a corporate event and much appreciated by all concerned. The ultimate benefit to the theatre world of the discovery of the remains of the Rose was an understanding of its lineaments and measurements that could be considered when the projected Shakespeare's Globe, whose plans were still in their infancy, would be built.

Theatre Set-Up itself had a very pleasant corporate entertainment of their own for their 30th anniversary in 2006 with a performance of *The Winter's Tale* in the Crush Room of the Royal Opera House, Covent Garden. The management there were very generous with a comparatively low hire fee, and they expressed pleasure that although there had been many opera rehearsals in the Crush Room, there had never been an actual performance there, certainly not of a play. Their arrangements on behalf of the company were immaculate, their waiters (serving wine or fruit juice), standing at strategic points in the room such as at the top of its entrance via the Grand Staircase and diplomatically refilling glasses when needed. Fortunately the sun shone brightly that day, streaming in through the upper windows of the Crush Room so that no stage lighting was needed, a change in the brightness of the chandeliers being all that was needed to mark the start and finish of the play and the interval. The play was dressed in the elaborate Elizabethan costumes which English National Opera had sold to Theatre Set-Up and which had originated from their past production of Benjamin Britten's opera "Gloriana". Glinting in the reflected light of the chandeliers, these costumes fortunately matched the splendour of the Crush Room. The Royal Opera House caterers supplied the delicious sandwiches for which they are famous, as well as coffee and service with plates and small forks for the company's birthday cake, made to match the colours of the Crush Room by a specialist in Enfield. There were 100 guests, representing Theatre Set-Up's venues and benefactors, all of whom regarded the occasion as a very special one. For Anne and the company it was a privileged experience to perform in such a beautiful location. All the arrangements for the event were made by the Royal Opera House management and staff with such kindness and consideration that it became easy to present the play there. It represented one of the many compensations for all the hardship the actors had endured over the years in performing in difficult venues in inclement weather.

Another compensating treat for the company was given by Sue and Phil Bowen in their home, Penlanole in Wales. They had built a living willow replica of Shakespeare's Globe theatre in one of their fields and engaged the Theatre Set-Up company to perform there.

But that was not all! They accommodated most of the actors for bed-and-delicious-breakfast in rooms in their large house and invited them all to an after-performance informal meal sitting around their kitchen table. It was a very warm, unique occasion, much valued by the actors who got a sense of how things might have been in Great House performances in Shakespeare's day.

Performing in Wales always seemed like going abroad to Anne. Crossing the border from England into Wales seemed indeed to be an international transit, as the English/Welsh road signs indicated the beginning of an exciting journey into a different country. Not only was the rugged mountainous terrain of Wales exotic but the Welsh people seemed very different from the English in the lilt of their speech and forthright expressions.

Anne had learned this during the 1980 performances of *As You Like it* in Plas Newydd which had been the company's first appearances in Wales and the enthusiastic company manager had coerced the actors to dress up in costumes and advertise the play in the streets of the town. Two actors, costumed in elegant eighteenth century velvet coats, rotated a banner advertising the play's performance to an ever interested audience. Two elderly gentlemen made their way to the front of the crowd,

"Will you be performing the play in Welsh?" they asked and were surprised and disappointed when told that the cast could only speak English.

MAINLAND EUROPEAN VENUES

In the mainland European venues where the company performed there was no question of the plays not being presented in English. That was what the audiences wanted and they were interested in the words so similar to their own, but sometimes considered archaic in modern English, in the original Shakespearean language versions of the plays that Anne had insisted should be performed in all the venues. There had been some discussion about possibly replacing now-archaic words with their modern equivalents which ironically would have made the language more difficult for audiences in mainland Europe to understand.

The generous hospitality which was also given to the company in Belgium, The Netherlands and Norway gave the perks the actors needed to get on with the exhausting tours. In Norway the Baroniet of Rosendal which hosted the performances was owned by the University of Oslo and the occasions were made into corporate celebrations with an opening banquet always attended by a government minister from one of the Scandinavian countries. At the first performance there (of *Hamlet*) in 1993, it was the Arts Minister who did the honours of welcoming the company to Norway. As she had been a professional singer, she concluded her speech with a song. Theatre Set-Up responded with a song from one of their singers and thereafter this became a tradition of the annual Norwegian banquets.

"You know that it is a tradition that you, as a guest speaker, should sing a song for us," Anne always said to the Scandinavian government ministers who were invited to the banquets. To everyone's pleasure they were all totally unfazed by this request and always sang for the assembled company, sometimes singing a folk song of their country for the benefit of the British actors. Anne wondered if British government ministers would be capable of such a response!

Another tradition that the actors upheld in Norway, much to Anne's disapproval, was swimming at night in the fjord near the Baroniet. However the Norwegian hosts always treated the actors to a trip to the local glacier and there they were challenged by the tough young Norwegians to swim in the glacier's freezing melt-water. The younger actors, keen to "fly the flag" for Britain, stripped off to their underwear and plunged, shrieking, into the icy water which they later claimed was very exhilarating, leaving their skin tingling for many hours afterwards.

All the actors were accommodated in the Baroniet's guest house, along with members of the audience. Breakfast was always an occasion for compliments from the audience for the actors. Many of the ingredients, especially the salad items, were grown in the Baroniet's gardens and all the cooked and baked items, especially the Baroniet's speciality pancakes, were prepared onsite. Beautiful young girls (which the Baroniet called "angels"), usually students of the university working in their vacations, carried out the variety of tasks required by the venue's function as host to the play with its audiences, as well as the daily visitors to the buildings and gardens of the Baroniet. Naturally these girls were of great interest to the young male actors and resulted in the marriage of one of the angels to an actor, creating a permanent link between the two countries.

The hospitality from the Baroniet usually began at the Bergen airport from where the actors and gear were taken by private boat, serving coffee and the famous Baroniet pancakes, to Rosendal in a spectacular journey along the Hardanger Fjord. In years when the private boat was not available the Fjord-bus served the purpose. However one year the only flight available from London to Bergen came in too late for either of these vessels. The only boat that would take on the journey was an intrepid old one that had been used for hunting seals and had sailed to the Arctic. An adventurous descent down a vertical ladder led to the main seating in the boat and although the actors relished this experience, Anne could not manage the ladder and stayed up above in a sheltered room off the deck.

As there was nowhere inside the boat where the gear and actors' luggage could be stored during the journey everything was left on the open deck. Unfortunately heavy rain beat down upon the boat as it made its way along the HardangerFjord towards Rosendal. This was no problem for the gear stored in hard cases, but the costumes were in soft cases which let in water. Upon arrival at the Baroniet, much drying out of these in the very early hours of the morning was required. Anne's case was also soft and she later discovered that all her clothes were damp, a circumstance which she ironically quite enjoyed, as the resulting coolness, although not good for her health, was welcome during the hot weather of that week!

The performances in the Baroniet of Rosendal were initiated by chance. In 1992 the company was performing in Cotehele in Cornwall and staying overnight in a local country hotel. Also staying there were Anne-Grete and Reidar Honerod who were on holiday from working on preparing the Baroniet in order to extend its tourist facilities. They were doing this on behalf of the University of Oslo who owned the castle. They arrived at the hotel too late to come to a performance in Cotehele but succumbed to the enthusiastic endorsement of Theatre Set-Up by the hotel's owners and asked Anne when they met her at the following morning's breakfast if the company could present some performances of their play during the next season. That the play would be *Hamlet* was providential, as the founder of the Baroniet was a nobleman called Rosencranz, which was also the name of a character in the play, thus providing a good feature for publicity.

Also pertinent for Anne was the fact that the maiden name of the mother of the Baroniet's Rosencranz was "Sinclair" and she had come from Scotland. Anne's grandfather was a Sinclair from the Shetlands in Scotland, so a family connection was imagined. When

Anne-Grete took Anne to view the tombs of the Sinclair/Rosencranz family in the local church, Anne extended this supposed fantasy.

"Hello cousins," she said, tapping the tombs in jest.

In future years she discovered that the Viking genealogy of her Shetland Sinclair ancestors was such that it might not have been a jest, as the Sinclair mother of the Rosendal Rosencranz was likely to have been a very distant relative!

The British Council, who had supported Theatre Set-Up's first performances in the Baroniet, recommended Theatre Set-Up to the administrators of Glimmingehus, a magnificent 16th century fortified tower/castle in Scania in Southern Sweden. Here the actors were again in the presence of amazing Vikings whose physical prowess astonished them. The most extraordinary of these was the woman custodian of the castle who was about eight months pregnant. In spite of this she climbed the steep stone staircases that led up to the performance space for the play on the castle's second floor with considerable alacrity. When Anne expressed concern about this the custodian replied:

"It is best. I find that when I am pregnant with my babies and I move slowly, when the baby comes out it is noisy, but when I run and move fast it is quiet and well-behaved when it arrives!"

Scania was a district renowned for its artists and the artistic values of its inhabitants. Anne found that this was not always a good thing. When a kindly person took Anne for a tour of the local Neolithic sites, she was puzzled by the seemingly incorrect orientation of the stones in a Neolithic tomb she was being shown.

"Where is East?" she asked her guide.

"Oh please, don't embarrass me," he protested, "the stones were moved around to make their arrangement look more attractive!"

The artistic values of the organisers of the actors' accommodation near Glimmingehus prevailed over all other considerations.

They were housed in accommodation which unfortunately did not comply with the British Equity (the actors' trade union) regulations.

"We chose that because the pictures there are good," explained the organisers as they transferred the actors to another location.

"Here the accommodation is correct but unfortunately there are no pictures. However the photographs on the walls are good," they beamed proudly.

All the indoor decoration of any buildings associated with Glimmingehus was beautifully designed, even the crockery that was used for the public in their café. This took precedence over the provision of an electric kettle for those preparing food for the public. Anne discovered this when she tried to make a hot drink one day there. The only way that this could be done was to heat water in a saucepan and dangerously pour it into a cup. The saucepan, of course, was sleek and well-designed!

One of the conditions in the contract between the organisers of the event and Theatre Set-Up was the provision of breakfast for all the actors. To supply this, the actors were taken to a restaurant many miles from their accommodation. Anne realised that the reason for this was that the pictures in the restaurant were excellent original paintings! The artists who created these works were invited to a spectacular party which was organised for the actors and local people in a beautiful modern building near the castle. The artists' works were displayed on the walls of the large rooms there and the actors were given a chance to talk to them about their work. The actors were impressed by the skill, modernity and freedom in their way of life and thinking of all the Swedish people that they met that evening and on all occasions during their performances at Glimmingehus.

The initial advent of Theatre Set-Up's programme of performances in mainland European venues also happened by chance.

In 1992 Anne was approached by several people while returning from the Isles of Scilly on the Scillonian ferry. They had seen the company's performance in St Mary's and noted that it did not distort the text and was not presented in any weird way – in other words it was a "straight" production. They were friends of the cultural officer in Offenburg, Germany, who had requested them to find a touring company who could provide "straight" performances of Shakespeare's plays for the town's school pupils and citizens.

"You cannot imagine the radical weirdness of performances of Shakespeare in Germany at the moment!" they exclaimed. "For example, in a recent performance of *King Lear*, the actress playing Goneril was required to urinate into a bucket onstage!"

As the scheduled Theatre Set-Up production for 1993 was to be *Hamlet*, a play most suitable for the Offenburg school pupils to study and then see it performed, the cultural officer arranged to hire the services of the company at the end of their UK season. Another venue en route to Offenburg (which was in the south of Germany) was needed to offset the cost of travel for such long distances from the UK. As performances in UK cathedrals were to be part of the Hamlet season, several performances for both schoolchildren and the general public were negotiated with the administrators of De Nieuwe Kerk in the centre of Amsterdam.

Anne was performing the role of Gertrude in this play, and on one occasion she did not have the strength to remove her stage makeup for her return to the digs (a local small hotel) after the performance in De Nieuwe Kerk. As she made her way with a woman friend through the Dam and along the roads bordering the canals on her way to her hotel she was surprised to be constantly asked how much she was charging for her (supposedly prostitute) services. Her friend decided that in consideration of the ambivalent moral atmosphere of the city where prostitutes advertised their wares in brothel front display windows, it was reasonable to suppose that Anne's Gertrude makeup made her appear like a local prostitute with her friend as her "Madam," touting for trade in the streets!

The performances in the Stadthalle theatre in Offenburg went well, Anne observing to the cultural officer that the schoolchildren in the audiences, responding to the wit in the play, seemed to understand it even better than many adults in UK audiences.

"You have very good teachers here!" she observed.

The Stadhalle always kept the same stage manager to look after the annual Theatre Set-Up performances and sometimes the same stage hands. The 1995 production of *A Midsummer Night's Dream* being performed that year in Offenburg was costumed in the period of 1895, honouring the 100th anniversary of the English National Trust (owner of many of the company's venues). The stage hands that year were Portuguese men who did not know the play. Having held the impression that Shakespeare was an icon of English "gravitas" literature, they were very surprised at the amount of rough comic action taking place on the stage – especially the actresses in their demure white dresses fighting viciously and stripping each other's clothes off down to the frilly long underwear, and the actor who was playing Bottom, suddenly wearing an ass's head and being embraced by the beautiful actress playing Titania, the Queen of the Fairies. They were, however, scarcely able to believe what happened in the *Pyramus and Thisbe* interlude in Act V. Enjoying the stage hands' reaction to their costumes in this part of the play, the actors presented themselves to them before their entrances on stage. The actor playing Flute was dressed as Thisbe in a white Victorian dress covered with frills and a bonnet covered with frills and flowers and the actor playing the wall was covered with canvas painted with bricks. The Portuguese could not believe it! However they refused to believe that this could be a genuine Shakespearean play when Anne appeared as Snug in the realistic costume of a lion, with the pipe (which the character she was playing never removed from his lips), protruding from the lion's mouth!

In following years in Germany wherever Theatre Set-Up presented their performances, the schools in the localities surrounding the venues would always select the company's forthcoming play as their curriculum Shakespeare play for that year. This even applied to the American schools for the USA in Heidelberg for the children of soldiers serving in the military stationed there. These schools went even further in putting on a number of performances of the scheduled play with all the pupils taking part. Before the 1996 performance of *Romeo and Juliet* as Anne went to the music desk, she was accosted by these young people, all shouting out enthusiastically the roles they had played in their own productions. Other members of the audience expressed concern over the noise these young people might make during the performance.

"Just you wait and see," she reassured them, "they know the play from having performed in it and they will comprise a silent, attentive audience." That was indeed the case, the young people completely engaged with a play that they had experienced themselves.

On the return from Offenburg to the UK in 1993, the company broke the long journey with an overnight stop in Ghent. The host and hostess of the B&B where Anne was staying were keen that the company should return in other years to present performances in Belgium.

"We will find venues and arrange them!" they declared.

With the help of the British Council and the enthusiastic hosts in the Ghent B&B, Anne ultimately arranged other venues in The

Netherlands and Belgium which would link up with the Offenburg performances and the most successful of these provided the basis for 19 years of performances in Mainland Europe.

One of the Belgium venues where the company performed for several years, Alden Biesen, had been well-known as the site of its castle, a building sadly diminished when Theatre Set-Up presented their annual plays in its modern theatre/hall. Evidently the reason for this was a disaster which had occurred some years earlier when the owner of the castle had wished to celebrate the sale of the castle to new prospective owners. As well as putting on a splendid banquet, he decided to light a fire in the magnificent fireplace in the room where the banquet was to be held. Unfortunately he did not check to see if the chimney above the fireplace had been cleaned and debris left there caught fire and subsequently burnt down most of the castle!

There were for Anne, however, very welcome aspects of the venue, as the hospitality included delicious meals and overnight beds for the actors in accommodation usually provided for visiting school-trip pupils. After the trauma of having one year taken school girls on an "away" geography field trip where the problems of both keeping them safely in their beds at night and in keeping the local boys away from their bedrooms seemed insurmountable, she resolved never to repeat the experience. Her caution was reinforced by the murder of an English schoolgirl in a school-trip dormitory by a local man in France. However she would not have worried about her pupils in the accommodation-for-school-parties she shared with the actresses at Alden Biesen. The dormitory included a bathroom with toilets so that no-one had any excuse to leave the room. Its window could not be accessed either from within or without and the bed for the teacher was right by the teacher-possessing-key-lockable door. Pupils (and in fact the actresses) would be safe and secure!

The Belgian venue which proved to be the most popular and enduring for the next 19 years was the Domein De Renesse in Malle. This beautiful castle was owned and run by the local community who also hosted the performances presented there each year by Theatre Set-Up, providing all the administration for the event and billeting the actors with members of the community. The castle room in which the plays were performed each year was cosy, inaugurating the style of setting which the company came to call **"Fireplace Acting"**. The fireplaces of European castles were always resplendent and provided a beautiful backdrop to any plays presented in front of them, mirroring what must have been conditions for Shakespeare's company, The King's Men, in their touring performances in private homes. The Domein De Renesse continued to host the plays to Theatre Set-Up's successors, The Festival Players, from 2012 onwards.

Anne was very embarrassed by the inappropriate behaviour of one of her actors (who had been difficult throughout the season), during a performance of *Twelfth Night* in the Brussels theatre venue, Ten Weyngaert. He kept disappearing from the wings and the dressing rooms between his cues and no-one could work out where he was going. Soon he was discovered. The management of the theatre had decided to put on the heaters in all areas of the theatre as autumn had arrived and the actor decided to take advantage of all of these in the backstage areas to dry out his personal clothes which he had washed in the hand-basins of the toilets! Needless to say it was his first, and (unless his behaviour changed) probably his last professional touring theatre engagement.

Over the years, performances in Ghent were held in several different venues in the city, the audiences mostly comprising school children. Accommodation was always guaranteed with the hosts of the B&B who had first arranged venues in Belgium and who continued to do the administration of several of the Belgian venues in future years. In fact their home in Baliestraat, Ghent was always declared as the home base for the Theatre Set-Up company in mainland Europe.

Theatre Set-Up was particularly proud of their inclusion in the annual listing of events in the "Agenda" of Brugge, in Belgium. The Brugge cultural officials scheduled the company's annual performances in the Biekorf Theaterzaal, an excellent small theatre in a road running off the main square with always the same skilled and friendly stage manager there to look after the production. As it was possible to find accommodation in a friendly hotel near the theatre and legal parking places for the company's van and car nearby, the whole visit to Brugge was very easy to organise and accomplish. The ease and pleasantness of this time in this lovely historic city provided a much-needed break for the actors from the trials of the tour. Always a perk for the actors were visits to the tourist sites of Brugge, including canal boat trips, art museums (especially to see the work of the Flemish painters including Jan van Eyck), the Michelangelo "Madonna and Child" sculpture, and wonderful restaurants. The city specialised in the production of lace which Anne always purchased for the company' costumes which thus held permanent mementos of this beautiful city and the excellent times Theatre Set-Up actors were able to enjoy there.

One of Anne's favourite venues in the whole tour of Theatre Set-Up's venues was Muiderslot, a castle 15 kilometres from Amsterdam in the Netherlands. This was a 15th century fairy-tale castle surrounded by a moat whose towers were topped with spires. The interior exactly reflected the paintings of Vermeer and there was a seat in the corners of the mullioned windows where Anne could play her musical instruments to accompany the play. In the hours before the play began Anne completed her Vermeer experience by mending costumes that required attention, trying to replicate the homely atmosphere created by Vermeer in his paintings. One Sunday morning after the Saturday evening performance, the company was invited to attend a concert that was being held in the castle. Anne attended and was talking to a Dutch lady whose appreciation of the Vermeer room equalled her own. This lady particularly liked the window seats.

"I play music and sew there," Anne happily told her.

The audiences in Muiderslot were particularly appreciative of Theatre Set-Up's performances there and always gave the play a standing ovation. The castle had small chairs for children which were always brought to the side and front of the "auditorium" for them. The children were always interested in the lighting of the candelabra which took place in the intervals. All the Netherlands castles defied the risk of a conflagration in lighting their candelabra with real fire. This was done with special equipment which reached up to the candelabra so that the staff did not have to climb up to them.

The smaller but equally beautiful Kasteel Doorwerth became a regular venue for Theatre Set-Up. Members of the castle's volunteers always billeted the actors and became great friends of the company. In all the Netherlands venues the administrators always invited the actors to join with the staff and volunteers in drinks and light refreshment after the performances. The hospitality did not stop there. Often presents, souvenirs of the castle which were on sale in the castle's shops, were given to the actors and Anne recalls performances in the lovely Kasteel Ammersoyen (where the company also performed), in the coasters given to her by the castle's custodians, as she uses them on her dining table in London.

The site chosen for the play in the Rijksmuseum Gevangenpoort Den Haag proved insufficiently popular to local people to attract a reasonable-sized audience, but the report of the play in the local paper caused amusement of the custodians of other Netherlands venues in its reflection of what they termed "Dutch fastidiousness". There was no discussion in this article of the play itself, but a fierce criticism was made of the venue's lack of service to the audience.

"There was nowhere for members of the audience to hang their coats," it complained!

In 1997 the young administrators of the MSS international Festival in Sarajevo (in Bosnia I Hercegovina) approached British Equity for the recommendation of a theatre company who could present a performance of a Shakespearean play in their forthcoming festival later that year. After the conflicts which had riven the countries in the former Yugoslavia, a ceasefire had been established and the MSS Festival organisers wished to celebrate the new peace and restart the festival. British Equity suggested that Theatre Set-Up would be able to take their 1997 production of *Twelfth Night* at the end of their UK and mainland tour to Sarajevo.

Thus a late autumn day saw the cast of this play, armed with its costume and props cases, waiting at the departures desk for a plane for Sarajevo. However Anne was suddenly called to discuss an issue concerning the flight with a representative of the plane company.

"Sadly the airport serving Sarajevo is closed today so I recommend that you all return home and wait to hear from us when it will be able to open again."

"Under no circumstances," responded Anne. "We have a play to perform in Sarajevo tomorrow night and I insist that you find a way to get us to Sarajevo this evening."

"Well, we will try. Perhaps we will be able to fly you to a city in a nearby country and take you by bus from there to Sarajevo."

Anne returned to the waiting cast with this announcement. They were surprised that there were any difficulties with Sarajevo airport, doubtless unaware of problems associated with the recent conflicts and consequently they became very nervous of the whole enterprise. Ultimately the airline officials decided to fly the company to the airport of Split in Croatia where a bus would be waiting to take them to Sarajevo. Anne was looking forward to meeting the casts of at least some of the other many countries who were sending their plays to the MSS Festival and expected that they would also have been sent to Split airport. However when the cast of Theatre Set-Up entered the bus waiting for them at Split airport, they found that they were the only ones occupying it, the administrators of the other companies still languishing in the departure lounges of their home airports.

The journey along the Dalmatian coast in Croatia and then through the devastated countryside of Bosnia I Hercegovina to Sarajevo was very instructive to the UK actors. Buildings along the road had been ruined during the conflicts, but if there was only one room remaining in a house, it was being lived in. Everywhere the efforts of the local people to rebuild the country and their lives were evident. The bus stopped at a café for a rest stop and food for the actors. Still unaware of the post-war problems of the country, the actors were disgruntled when they were told that there was no toilet paper available in the toilets! The roads in many places were full of holes but the bus made its way steadily to Sarajevo and took the actors and their gear to the headquarters of the MSS Festival. By this time it was midnight, but all the MSS officials were assembled in the main room of the building, very wary of the fierce UK team who had been the only one to force the airline to find an alternative way to bring them to Sarajevo. They were very consoled when they met the cheerful, relaxed actors, chatting happily to them about the wonderful journey.

The UK contingent was allotted two guides, one Muslim, one Christian to assist them throughout their stay, and they were all given excellent accommodation in hotels and a "per diem" (daily) food allowance, according to the rules of British Equity. All the cast were full of admiration for the organisers of the MSS Festival, bringing theatre companies to Sarajevo from all over the world. They were surprised to discover that they were all very young, many of them university students, resuming their courses after the conflicts. Many of them were obviously badly scarred, both physically and mentally. One of the guides who was helping the UK actors was so traumatised by her wartime experiences that she found it difficult to eat. The buildings, including the theatres where the performances were held, were pock-marked with bullet holes, and many buildings were completely or partly ruined. The *Twelfth Night* performance went according to plan except that the simultaneous translation from English into the local language went wrong, and many in the audience, unfamiliar with the play, could not understand it, especially as the plot involves action involving look-alike twins!

The return journey for the UK cast was very sad as they were leaving behind newly-made friends whom they had identified were in a very vulnerable state. There were plenty of tears shed on the plane leaving Sarajevo. Anne and one of the actresses maintained contact with the guides into future years, exchanging greeting cards at Christmas and the New Year.

CHAPTER 4

"ALL FOR YOUR DELIGHT/ WE ARE NOT HERE"

NOBLE HERITAGE AND HOSPITALITY

Anne was always able to purchase excellent greetings cards and presents to be given to the company's mainland European hosts (in response to their generosity to the casts) from the shops of the UK venues. As the cast's changing room in Ingatestone Hall, Essex, was in their shop and as the items for sale represented the venue's history dating from the time of Henry VIII, Anne usually bought her presents there. For the children of the company's European hosts, Viking-style toys from the Isle of Man's Peel Castle, and toy weaponry from English Heritage castles was also ideal. Of course Viking-style toy gifts for the children of the company's UK hosts purchased in Norway's Bergen airport also brought squeals of delight and hours of play for UK children. They were thus happily enjoying a shared Viking heritage (which was tangibly demonstrated in the toys) with the mainland European children.

Not of a Viking but of a Norman heritage, Holme Pierrepont in Nottinghamshire enjoyed an even more ancient history than Ingatestone Hall, the recorded ancestry of its owners going back even further through the centuries. The outdoor performance site was protected from wind by enclosing trimmed high hedges. Unfortunately the right and left backstage areas giving access to this were in fairly high grass, resulting in much sneezing from members of the cast who suffered from hay fever. These unhappy few were very glad when forecast rain scheduled the plays to be performed inside the beautiful hall in its long gallery which was often used as a wedding feast venue.

Of similar high historic pedigree was the venue, Chatsworth House, in Derbyshire. However the expanse of its magnificent gardens in which performances were held presented problems in those years before the company had pavilion-style changing tents which could be brought onto the right and left of the stage area. In those early years changing into initial costumes from street clothes and then into the different costumes needed to represent the different characters of the play needed to take place behind buildings or vegetation as near as possible to the stage area. In the Chatsworth gardens these areas were very far from the performance area and actors had to run off, change into another costume and then run on again in order to perform on cue. On one occasion it proved impossible for an actor to do this and an embarrassing pause in the stage action was threatened. Rising to save the situation, a senior actor, Gordon Fleming, sallied forth and recited one of the Shakespearean sonnets that he had prepared for his forthcoming programme of European recitals. It was incidents like this which motivated the local press officer to write in his review of the performance that it boasted "leather-lunged actors".

Another senior actor, Frank Jarvis, was wandering in the outskirts of the main house of Chatsworth, looking for somewhere to fill his water bottle when the current Duchess of Devonshire saw him and asked if she could help him. When she heard that he was looking for the ingredients of the cast's interval tea she disappeared and then kindly presented him with a bottle of milk from the ducal refrigerator. This kitchen appliance was well-stocked for the many guests staying at Chatsworth House. One of these was the current poet laureate, Sir John Betjeman who commented to Frank Jarvis after the play on how much he had enjoyed the performance and how he admired the speed of the actors getting from the changing areas onto the stage.

"At such moments," replied Frank, rephrasing one of Betjeman's own poems, "We think 'Come friendly German bombs and drop on Chatsworth!'"

On another occasion a house guest who was a member of the 1984 UK government tottered across the lawn toward the play holding a glass of wine, expecting to be allowed to watch the play free-of-charge, but Frank demanded that he pay for his ticket!

The members of the aristocracy who had previously owned Kedleston Hall, Derby and who, after it was taken over by the National Trust, lived there in the Family wing, were much taken by the company's performances presented at the Palladian North front of the Hall, using its sweeping staircases and retreating behind its central lower door to their changing areas. All members of the company declared, in the years that they performed there, that it was by far the easiest venue to perform in. It was possible to drive the company van right up to the North Front, to unload the gear there and set costumes and props up inside the vast room behind the lower front door, to set up lighting and sound equipment in front of the building and then to drive the van away to its parking spot. To pack up was just as quick, reversing the process. All this was possible due to the excellence of the National Trust administrator. The additional welcome given to the cast by the venue's heritage nobility made this a favourite venue.

The actors had learnt the truth of the saying "Noblesse oblige" in several historic houses. They had always been treated with the ultimate courtesy and consideration by the aristocratic owner, 2nd Viscount De L' Isle, of Penshurst Place. At the venue in Ingatestone Hall, the 18th Baron of the peerage title, Lord Petre, until recently HM Lord Lieutenant of Essex, whose ancestors had owned the manor since the time of Henry VIII, also gave an excellent example of this principle. Devoid of all snobbishness which his exalted status could have warranted, he rolled up his sleeves, and assisted by his son Dominic, put out the chairs for the audiences, packing them away afterwards. He served refreshments in the interval, functioned as "Box Office" at the entrance to the performance area and restored the site to its daytime order after the performances. Aware of the distress of audiences caught in rained-on performances and of the subsequent difficulty the cast would have in drying out the damp costumes and lighting equipment, he made a large inside room available for any performances on evenings which were forecast to be wet. He was the complete, considerate, kind, unassuming gentleman.

The casts had admired the grace and etiquette of the Baron and Baroness de Potesta, descended from thirteen generations of owners of the Chateau De Waleffe in southern Belgium where Theatre Set-Up performed for several years. Called by everyone "Le Baron", he showed particular care of the play's audience members, providing them with a screened-off hanging space for their outdoor coats and giving them refreshments before the play. This was particularly appreciated by one lady in the audience who commented:

"On mange, on boit!"

He was a particularly gracious host to the British Ambassador to this part of Belgium who had come to enjoy seeing the Theatre Set-Up "flying the flag" in his territory. "Le Baron" not only served him with refreshments after his long journey to the performance, but took him on a guided tour of the chateau after the play had ended. The women in Theatre Set-Up's cast were very impressed with the gracious style of the Baroness, whose elegant posture and discreet welcome to all members of the audience created a special atmosphere for the play.

In the Cornwall stately home of Pencarrow, Lady St Aubyn demonstrated a noble generosity to the cast each year that they performed there. She would appear at their dressing tents at the side of the magnificent raised lawn stage with welcome trays of hot soup, bread rolls and mugs of tea. Often there would be additional treats such as home-baked Cornish pasties and cakes. On damp, cool evenings this was most welcomed by the cast. In the typical laid-back style of the English aristocracy, her manner was unassuming and modest.

Generous hospitality was also a feature of the owners of Kentwell Hall, Sussex, who were not members of the aristocracy. They always provided the theatre company's casts with a full meal in the long "picnic interval" which audiences enjoyed at the performances. Similar hospitality for the casts was given by the estate of Tresco Abbey Gardens, whose owner, Mr Robert Dorrien-Smith, was the company's patron. Hospitality for the cast like this at venues such as Buckden Towers, Cossington Manor, Ford Park Cumbria, Lacock Abbey, La Seigneurie, Sark, The Lost Gardens of Heligan,

Mottisfont Abbey, Penlanole, St Gabriel's Church, Cwmbran, Stourhead, Baroniet Rosendal Norway, Glimmingehus Sweden, Château De Prangins, Switzerland, Domein De Renesse, Belgium, Kasteel Doorwerth, Kasteel Ammersoyen, and Muiderslot, in the Netherlands, lightened the touring schedule for the actors and made the seasons memorable.

The custodians of Dunster Castle, Somerset, rose to the occasion in providing food for the cast of the first performance there in 1983. The distance between the departure point of London and the castle had been miscalculated and the actors arrived at the venue almost in time to set up and perform the play, not having had time to eat. Rushing to her freezer, the custodian's wife, Grace Beamish, found enough frozen sausages to feed the numbers of the cast. Rapidly defrosting and cooking the sausages, placing them in chunks of delicious buttered bread and adding slices of home-made cake, she plied the starving actors with much-appreciated fuel for their performance. In future years of course adequate time was allowed for the journey to the castle, a beautiful venue at Lacock Abbey being scheduled between London and Dunster, the actors finding time to eat an excellent lunch in the famed Red Lion pub in the historic Lacock main street, the scene of many period films.

A STRESSFUL JOURNEY

Journey times to venues were often very stretched. The most challenging of these was from London, leaving Oakwood in the company van and car at 8am, travelling to Dover to catch the ferry from there to Calais and from Calais travelling to the Domein De Renesse in Oostmalle, North Belgium, for the 8pm start of a performance. Hospitality and efficiency from the Belgium hosts made this possible for most years, but in 2005 this was made difficult by severe storms which threatened to prevent the ferry from sailing from Dover. Anne tackled the people running the ferry:

"You have to run the ferry. We are due to perform in Belgium this evening. The reputation of the UK is at stake here. It is not only football matches in Europe which condition the prestige of our country – our travelling theatre companies do that also!"

Against their better judgement the ferry company allowed the ferry to go to Calais. What a journey! The motion of the ferry in the storm was so great that crockery and glasses, if put on tables or counters, were swept off and broken; it was impossible for anyone to sit on a bench or chair on board without holding on to something to prevent sliding to the floor, and a journey which normally took one and a half hours, lasted for four hours! The port authorities in Calais were understandably not expecting any ferry to have made the crossing and were astonished when the shattered vessel arrived. Rushing in their vehicles to Oostmalle, the actors were able to perform to a patiently-waiting audience only one hour late!

It was always a rush to get to Oostmalle and this led to narrowly-averted disaster in 2011 when Anne was doubling her role of Margaret in *Much Ado About Nothing* with that of the friar who was supposed to try to marry Hero and Claudio before the latter cancelled the marriage. She was so stressed by the fatigue of the journey that in her haste she mixed up her lines and jumped to the end of the scene. Suddenly she realised what she had done:

"I've forgotten to try to marry them! The whole plot has been lost!" she silently despaired.

So she jumped back into the beginning of the scene and proceeded with the marriage ceremony. The cast, who had been alarmed by the possibility of losing the whole plot of the play, jumped back with her and thus Claudio rudely stopped the marriage with his false accusations against Hero and the play proceeded as Shakespeare had intended.

COSTUME EVENTS

Often actors performing different roles within the play became confused about which character they were next due to perform and they changed into the wrong costume. For this reason it became a rule-of-thumb that no-one should have to change costume alone and that all actors, as well as assisting each other in their costume changes, should know the order in which everyone should be taking their different roles in the play. Unfortunately in the 2002 performances of the final scene of *As You Like It*, it was not possible for anyone to help Anne for her costume change into the friar who, it was decided, (in the absence of anyone who was available to play Shakespeare's casting of Orlando and Oliver's other brother) would announce that the wicked Duke who had been on his way to wreak havoc upon everyone, had been converted to pacifism by an "old religious man". If you run a Shakespeare theatre company, you need two friars' costumes. Anne had made these two garments, capacious enough to fit anybody, for the 1977 performances of *Romeo and Juliet.* The problem was, that as they were so large, it was easy to mistake one of the sleeves for the neck. On the first night of the 2002 season Anne ran off in her character of Audrey (who had no lines in the end of this scene so could easily shuffle off stage) and proceeded to try to get into the friar's costume which could easily fit on top of her Audrey outfit. Try as she might she could not find the neck of the friar's costume, always putting her head through one of the capacious sleeves. There was a very long silence on stage, the actors there very aware of the problem going on in the stage right tent. Ultimately she got her head through the right gap and rushed on stage with the announcement needed to end the play. On the second night the actors sang a reprise of the song delivered by the character of Hymen about the joys of marriage and Anne managed to change into the friar's costume in time for her entrance. On the third night she did not succeed and gave up the attempt, throwing the costume off and rushing on as Audrey, announcing that she had just seen an old religious man who had told her about his conversion of the wicked Duke.

Aware of the problems of unassisted changing into the friar's costume, the off-stage cast of *Much Ado About Nothing* in 2011 made sure that they helped Anne get her head through the neck of the friar's costume before she entered as the friar due to marry Hero and Claudio. This was usually successful, but in the venue of Great Bidlake Manor, in Devon, they accidentally put the costume on her back to front. She discovered this when she tried to put the hood up. There was no time to start again with the costume change so she twisted the hood around to the back and tied a belt around the waist to keep the costume straight. When she got onto the stage the cast there could see exactly what had happened and were contorted through the scene with the effort of suppressing their laughter. As it is a very serious part of the play this reserve was necessary. However the gravity was lost when they made their exits from the scene and relieved peals of incongruous laughter rang out from the changing tents. **Both friars' costumes were considered to be hazards which should be approached with extreme caution!**

One year Anne slept among the costumes. She was teaching in a London college at the time and performing each night in Wallington Hall Northumberland. When she had her half-day off from college she drove her car at high speed to the venue and parked it there. The cast's green room into which the costumes were stored happened to have a camp-bed in it, so in order to save time and effort at the end of the first performance, Anne changed from her costume into her night wear and, settling down onto the camp-bed, said good-night to the cast (some of them very envious of her privilege in be allowed to do this) as they left for their digs. When she was woken up occasionally during the night by the cold, at first she could not work out why she was surrounded by all the costumes, but soon she remembered and endured the situation. The next morning she was up at 4 am, washed, dressed into her college clothes and driving off to Newcastle-upon-Tyne railway station to catch the first train to London which left at 6 am. In the late afternoon she took the express train to Newcastle-upon-Tyne station, drove to the venue, arriving just in time to change into costume and to go onstage. In subsequent years Mrs Jennings, the member of the Trevelyan family living in an apartment in Wallington Hall itself, (which had been gifted by the family to the National Trust), invited her to stay in her guest bedroom while Theatre Set-Up performed there, sparing her the necessity of sleeping in the chilly costume store room.

STAYING AT THE VENUES

The curators of other National Trust venues often were kind enough to invite her to stay in their apartments. The curator of Hanbury Hall went one better than that and decided that she should sleep in one of the curtained four-poster beds in the stately home itself. It was a claustrophobic but wonderfully rare experience!

Accommodation was provided for the actors in buildings onsite at the National Trust property, Sudbury Hall. Inmates from a local prison were employed to do some outdoor work on the site during one of the early mornings while the actors were staying there. One of the beautiful actresses, wearing a long-sleeved capacious white cotton nightgown, went to the door of the building where she was staying to breathe in the morning air, and she noticed the workmen. Thinking that they were regular National Trust employees, she stood still in the doorway in her white nightdress and waved enthusiastically in greeting to them. It must have been quite an unexpected perk for them away from their prison on that summer morning.

MUSIC

Often songs would need to be put into the plays in order to cover necessary costume changes. As long as these were relevant to the play in subject matter and from the period in which the play was being costumed, the audiences liked this. Musical instruments needed to be appropriate also. The first of these which Anne bought and learnt to play was a lute. It had not been her intention at all to embark on the possession and playing of such a prestigious instrument, but circumstances dictated otherwise. In 1978 The National Trust houses of Wallington Hall and Beningbrough Hall asked for Theatre Set-Up to present a Shakespearean performance at their venues during the summer of 1979. At the site visit Anne made to Beningbrough Hall in the autumn of 1978, the man in charge of events for the region was a nationally well-known musical expert whom The National Trust had lured into their service.

"What music do you use?" he asked Anne. For the previous two productions there had been little music, but what there was had been played on recorders.

"We use live music played on our own instruments," responded Anne.

As the play to be performed was *Twelfth Night* whose script features instrumental music and songs, Anne knew that she had to acquire an early music instrument for the task in order to satisfy her National Trust hosts. She found out that a mandolin represented the treble section of a lute, so off she went to a store which sold musical instruments to buy one.

"What do you want it for?" asked the expert selling these instruments.

"For professional performances of Shakespeare's *Twelfth Night* in Forty Hall, Enfield and several National Trust houses in the North."

Standing in front of the mandolins so that she could not get at them, this expert said to his employee:

"Fetch a lute!"

The young lad did so and came forth with an enormous lute.

"This is what you should play," he declared, brooking no argument.

"Who can teach me please?"

"The Early Music Centre, Holland Park."

So every Wednesday evening for several years Anne enjoyed tuition at this excellent organisation with a wonderful lute teacher, and Theatre Set-Up's venues at which she played the lute (amplified of course), were very pleased with it, even when they understood that she was playing very simple tunes! They did not mind what music was played as long as it was on a real period instrument performed by someone in a costume appropriate to the play.

Sometimes members of the audience were interested in the music that Anne was playing.

"Where did you find that early music?" asked a man in the audience of an outdoor performance at beautiful Lacock Abbey on one occasion.

"In my Adelaide University lecture notes," replied Anne. "One day our brilliant lecturer, Dr Jack Peters, came grumpily into our lecture with a great pile of papers with examples of early music which he had reproduced for us on a gestetner over the weekend. He complained bitterly that while he was stuck inside doing that, his family were enjoying swimming at the seaside in idyllic sunny weather. Sadly he has died, but I think that if he could have heard the music he gave me on that day being played at all these beautiful heritage sites, he would have felt compensated for the loss of that weekend's swim with his family."

Making use of much later music, the play to be toured and performed in 1981 was *Much Ado About Nothing* which was to be set and costumed in the Victorian period. Anne's teaching colleague had an antique portable organ which she volunteered to enter into the service of the production. It became like another member of cast, with its need to be very carefully handled! Anne wore an over-fringed Victorian-style costume which the cast called a "lampshade" and before the play began and in the role of the play's house musician, she would play music from that era, particularly popular songs with which the audience could sing-along.

This whole process went into overdrive during the several weeks of performances held in The Pump Room, Bath. The grand piano which was played during the day as part of a trio to entertain the customers taking tea in The Pump Room could not be removed from the stage during the performance of the play in the evenings. In order to rationalise its presence there, Anne decided to play it before the start of the performances in her role as the play's house musician, whose standards of performance, like hers, would not have to be those of a professional pianist. In order to emphasise the features of this role, at the end of each piece that she played she would rise and bow in response to the applause, all the fringes of her costume shaking. Over the weeks the standard of her performance improved so that she was actually presenting an improvised piano concert for about an hour before the play was about to begin when she would bow to the audience, leave the stage and start playing for them on the little organ. After a while the cast noticed this "upstaging" of their performance of the play and were slightly peeved! However Anne was always secretly pleased that she had been able to present mini-concerts on the beautiful grand piano on the stage of The Pump Room, Bath. **It was a testament to the benefits of performing in role.**

The next musical instrument to be used by the Theatre Set-Up company came to them through their performance on the Scillonian island of Tresco where Celtic music was being played on a folk harp in local concerts by Tresco Abbey's gardener, Peter Clough. This had been made on the island by one of its residents and Anne ordered one to be made for the company's projected performance of *The Tempest* in 1982, the following year. This was duly done but, alas, its neck, which had been elaborately carved, broke when it was tuned by its maker. Distraught, he resolved never to make another harp and recommended that Anne should purchase a plainer folk harp in a shop in Brighton. There Anne bought the harp which she would love to play for many years. It encompassed several octaves of strings which were basically in the key of C major, but pins beside the top of the strings could raise their pitch by a semitone. This made the harp very versatile and Anne found that she could not only play the Celtic music for which the harp was designed but tunes from Mozart's operas and those of many other composers.

She had always wanted to find a dulcimer as it is mentioned in the script of *A Midsummer Night's Dream.* One day in 1990 the friend with whom she was staying during performances at Trelissick Gardens, Cornwall, came rushing into her room:

"They have a hammered dulcimer for sale in the shop!"

So off Anne went to purchase this dulcimer and as she paid for it she noticed another much smaller instrument modestly displaying itself by the dulcimer's side.

"What is that beautiful instrument?" she asked, experiencing love at first sight for it, "and do you have a contact number for its maker?"

"It is a psaltery and here is the phone number of its maker."

When phoned, this person told Anne that pictures from the Middle Ages and Renaissance periods show angels playing psalteries with their right hands which they hold tightly to their chests with their left hands as they walk. He explained that to hold the instrument in that way gives it resonance from the player's chest cavity and that is how it should be played.

"Then I shall play it that way when we process into the performance this evening!" exclaimed Anne. She informed the actors (who had been difficult that day) that she was bringing a new member of cast into the production that night. Nervous about who that might be and how they would be affected by this newcomer, they were re-assured when Anne joined their processing onto the stage playing the psaltery which turned out to be the new addition to their number!

Although the instrument had only 15 strings and no pins to raise them by a semitone like the folk harp, Anne found that she could play much music on it (with only her right hand) that she normally performed on the harp. The casts of the plays were delighted with this as even in its protective flight case it was easy to carry and store in the van. (Over the years Anne had learnt to have all her musical instruments carried and stored in flight cases. These protected the instruments in a temperature-controlled enclosure so that their strings did not break and the body of the instrument was not damaged.)

The purchased dulcimer had a much shorter performance life, although with its 50 odd strings it was capable of performing most music. Anne found it difficult to keep all its strings in tune in outdoor environments and it was quite cumbersome to transport, needing a small supporting table as both her hands were needed to wield the two hammers required to play it. It proved invaluable for the performance of Slavic music at a Slavic-themed performance of *Twelfth Night* (justified as the country of Illyria in which Shakespeare set the play is the former Slavic Yugoslavia). However, where it came into its own was in Victorian- themed performances of *Measure for Measure* and *A Midsummer Night's Dream*, the antique organ no longer needing to be taken on tour. Evidently in the nineteenth and early twentieth centuries this instrument was used in homes for domestic music-making and in the streets by musicians who propped it up on an attached pole. The Mendelssohn incidental music to *A Midsummer Night's Dream* was easily played on it and the waver that characterised music (especially the accompaniment to songs) of the period seemed to have stemmed from the vibrating nature of the strings played by its two hammers. It was quite an enlightening discovery.

When Anne was playing the dulcimer in a performance of *A Midsummer Night's Dream* in the Salle Paroissiale, Limpertsberg, Luxembourg for an audience of unruly school pupils, she accidentally knocked over her music stand and the music went flying to the floor.

A gasp of pleasure went up from the school pupils who expected that she would have to spoil the scene by stopping the play to pick up the music. However it was near the end of the tour's season and she could actually play the music without reference to the music stand's contents, and with a triumphant smile to the pupils, continued uninterrupted. They were very disappointed, having hoped to score a Luxembourg triumph over inadequate English actors.

In 1987 when Theatre Set-Up presented *The Two Gentlemen of Verona* in La Seigneurie, Sark, in the Channel Islands, a special musical trick was played which mystified the audience. Good use was made during the performance of the tower in La Seigneurie, the character of Silvia realistically appearing at its top in the scene where her father has imprisoned her in a tower away from the courtship of her would-be lover, Valentine. The actor singing the song: "Who is Silvia? What is she/ That all our swains commend her?" also decided to perform from the top of this tower. As this song needed to be accompanied by the lute, while Anne as lutenist was firmly established beside the stage area below, there could have been problems in coordinating the lute and singer for the song. However the actor playing the role had the gift of perfect pitch and to the surprise of everyone, began his song on the same note as the one played on the lute. His skill in this way often gave pleasure to audiences.

THE JOY OF GARDENERS, GARDEN EVENTS AND WHISKY

The Tresco Abbey gardener who led Anne to the discovery of the joys of playing a folk harp was, in his indispensable kindness to the company, typical of his kind throughout the country. The cast always rejoiced when they discovered that they were to perform in a garden venue as they knew that the gardeners would be their allies in preparing, performing and packing up the production. The first of these was at Forty Hall, Enfield where not only the gardeners and the rangers but the Parks department helped them, the latter often supplying them with plants to augment their settings. During the first week of Theatre Set-Up's daily rehearsals on the West lawn of Forty Hall, the gardeners were not pleased to see the lawn becoming worn from the constant tread of the actors' feet. However soon they began to rejoice in observing that the moles whose holes had punctuated the lawn had been chased away by those very same feet!

The gardeners in the Rookery in Streatham Common assisted in ways which became typical throughout the UK. Costumes, props and lighting gear had to be stored overnight when several performances were scheduled in this venue. The only place available for this was in the gardeners' huts which were kindly made available. When rain soaked the costumes in the first performance, the gardeners kindly dried out the costumes for the following ones. This procedure was well-followed in the Harlow Gardens in Yorkshire, where the gardeners took all costumes into their glasshouses and dried them off there. In Tresco they took responsibility for the packing-up of all the costumes and gear into a container which, in days following the performance, they would take to the Scillonian ferry for the actors to retrieve at Penzance. This was really necessary as the actors' return to their digs in the neighbouring island of St Mary's after the performance had to be taken in the night when only a passenger-carrying commissioned launch was available. This 20 minute journey by launch through the darkening sky amid glinting Atlantic waves (especially as all the production's gear had been left behind in capable hands), became Anne's favourite part of all the tour.

Mike Nelhams, the head gardener of Tresco Abbey from the late 1980s, introduced several other excellent garden venues to the company through his gardening associates. Thus Theatre Set-Up came to perform in The Lost Gardens of Heligan in Cornwall, in the Ventnor Botanic Garden in the Isle of Wight and in Abbotsbury SubTropical Garden, Dorset. In all of these the gardeners made life easy for the cast and audiences. Performances in the Ventnor Botanic Garden were very special. Theatre Set-Up had performed in other Isle of Wight venues since 1982 and built up a very loyal audience there who turned up at 5.30pm to read the play's programme notes and to secure places to put their folding chairs at the front of the audience area. The Ventnor Botanic Garden venue, deep down into the garden, with the sound of waves from the nearby sea coast humming in the background, seemed to be like Prospero's Island in *The Tempest* and the magic of that imagined realm also defined the Ventnor scene. The children who came to performances there were always brought to the front of the audience area and the tangible magic of the site seemed to possess them in their rapt attention to the play.

This contrasted with the children in The Rookery, Streatham Common in South London, a park whose beauty the Dutch artist Vincent Van Gogh had celebrated in a drawing of part of it while he was resident nearby. This lovely site for the plays, held in a natural amphitheatre with a lawn sloping down to a flattened area backed by a garden, had a parallel lawn running alongside it which children from the audience found irresistible to run down during the performance. However, from its first performances there in 1980, the venue always had local administrative support, large, enthusiastic audiences (tolerant of the running children), and it remained the most long-lasting venue of Theatre Set-Up, continuing after 2011 to be included in the tours of the follow-on company, The Festival Players.

It was important to locate the play in all the venues in such a way that the backdrop focused on the most beautiful view the venue had to offer. Often gardens in front of orangeries provided very successful settings. Immediately outside the Orangery of Saltram House, Devon, and inside the Orangery of Kenwood House, North London were lovely locations. However this could go badly wrong. As it was not possible to present the play on the newly-planted grass outside the Orangery of Kew Gardens, the play had to be performed inside it. Unfortunately the echo which resonated back and forth from its glass panelling, destroyed the sound of the play to the dissatisfaction of any members of the audience sitting more than a foot away from the stage area!

From 1982 onwards, Theatre Set-Up performed annually in the garden amphitheatre in the grounds of Chiswick House, London. In 1981, while walking in the grounds during the hours before a performance which the company was to present on the steps in front of the house itself, Anne found this terraced site looking forlorn and bedraggled, centred by a lake overgrown with weeds with a small temple building at its far end. Since one of the aims of Theatre Set-Up was to bring unkempt sites into life, she decided that future performances should revive the beauty of the site and perform there. On contacting the gardeners she discovered that they were very willing to accede to her request and each year they raked the growths from the lake, weeded the terraces and cleaned out the temple. After the performance a gardener would come on his bicycle to lock up the site and in gratitude and in memory of her Scottish father (who had been very active in establishing the company), Anne would give him a bottle of whisky to be shared by the gardeners of the grounds. As the venue was under the one of the flight paths leading to Heathrow Airport, detailed arrangements had to be made to the tour schedule in order to ensure that the performances held there were at times when the noise from overhead planes was minimal. Most urgently, the play had to be arranged so that the interval occurred at 9pm, the time when Concorde flew directly over Chiswick. Unaware of this fact when the first Theatre Set-Up performance was presented on the site, the actors were astonished when Concorde soared overhead during the first half of the play, blocking out all sight of the sky while its reverberating engines drowned all speech on stage. However Frank Jarvis was up to the task required. Stopping the play with a wave of his hand that commanded all the audience to gape like him skyward, he exclaimed:

"I never thought Leonardo Da Vinci would get that thing up!"

On another occasion when, in spite of the carefully arranged schedule, Concorde soared overhead, one of the cast shouted above the din:

"Did you see that great big bird?"

In order to minimise plane noise during the rest of the play, Anne had to have contact with the administration of Heathrow Airport to determine which runways would be used at what times and then she had to schedule the Chiswick performances accordingly. So that residents beneath the runways were not constantly aggravated by planes flying immediately over them, alternate runways were used for different flight paths, with changes effected every few hours. Anne established with the Heathrow Airport administrators that the timing of the play would be affected by the change in flight paths taking place every day at 6pm and the less noisy flight path would be that where planes landed on runway 27A. She consequently arranged performances at Chiswick House Temple Amphitheatre to take place on those dates when the planes were landing on runway 27A after 6pm. Other performances in other venues had to fit around that!

Imagine her horror and disgust one year when, in spite of all this trouble, noisy planes, obviously on the flight path bound for runway 27B, were flying immediately over the play. She rushed to the shed of the friendly gardeners.

"Can you believe it?" she cried to them, "Please can I use your phone?"

"You are using runway 27B when you should be using 27A," she shouted down the phone at the Heathrow Control Tower.

"We have to change runways to make some alterations to 27A" they replied.

"Do your alterations another time. Go back to 27A. **Take your planes away from my temple!"**

It was too late to change the planes' routes for that night, but during future performances of Theatre Set-Up in the Temple Amphitheatre of Chiswick House Gardens, the Heathrow Airport administration kindly ensured that 27A was the runway always used by the planes landing after 6pm!

Another venue which the Theatre Set-Up performances caused to be tidied up, followed by a grateful gift of whisky to the gardeners, was the garden outside Westmere in the grounds of The University of Birmingham where the Shakespeare Institute originally had its library and study rooms. This small token of memorial whisky was the procedure followed after all the garden venues, and the gardeners always drank to Anne's father's memory in the week following the performances. This was so appreciated that Anne eventually gave all the people running the venues a father-remembered bottle. The boot and part of the back seat of Anne's car was always kept full of whisky bottles (or red wine for those who did not like whisky). In order to keep the bottles intact the car had to be driven very carefully!

THE HISTORICAL RESONANCE OF SOME VENUES

The historical resonance of some of the venues where the company performed gave the actors a chilling frisson. This was particularly the case in the ancient Roman theatre of Verulamium in St Albans. As the actual stage was in ruins, the Theatre Set-Up performances there were staged in the Orchestra, the circular area beyond that where the Chorus in traditional classic plays had performed. The actors sited their changing areas at the tops of the right and left Vomitoria, large ramps which gave access to the Orchestra. As they progressed down these they realised that not only were they treading in the steps of actors who were performing there nearly two thousand years before, but also in those of people about to be executed in the arena!

Less chilling but also memorable were the ruins of Kenilworth Castle where the ruined remains still existed of parts of the castle (in particular the fireplaces) where Robert Dudley, the Earl of Leicester, entertained Queen Elizabeth I. Also the imagined shadow of a very young Shakespeare was cast there, as it is supposed that he was brought there as a child by his father to at least one of the entertainments presented by Leicester to his Queen. In *A Midsummer Night's Dream* Shakespeare describes, in words spoken by Oberon, that he heard "a mermaid on a dolphin's back" (Act I scene 1, line 150), a scene which replicates exactly one of the items in a theatrical fantasy staged on a lake beside the castle which had been created by Leicester for the entertainment of Elizabeth.

Performances in the historic Georgian Theatre Royal, Richmond, Yorkshire, always brought a sense of the theatrical memory of the actors who had performed there for centuries and the hundreds of plays that had been presented on its stage. Seating for the audience in the stalls was on benches and sometimes people fell off them during a performance. There were chairs in the boxes, some of them so close to the stage that actors would sometimes directly address members of the audience seated in them. The stage itself was slanted quite steeply and the stage door gave direct access to the path outside along which vehicles were permitted to unload the plays' gear before being taken away to be parked elsewhere. Opposite this door was a pub whose side door opened upon this path. After one performance when the actors were preparing the costumes to be loaded into the van by hanging them on costume rails by the door, several very drunk young men came out of the pub and into the theatre, and tried to put some of the costumes on themselves. Chased off by the stage manager, they complained that the clothes were "very old fashioned".

Glastonbury Abbey was a very special performance place, charged with spiritual energy. When Theatre Set-Up first performed there in the mid 1990's, the cast were alarmed that during the performance all their mirrors were somehow broken. The performance there during the following year had to be cancelled after attempting to battle against winds and rain which threatened to destroy costumes and lighting gear. A person living in Glastonbury who had psychic knowledge commented that there was a person in the cast (whom they identified) whose cynicism was creating negative vibes on the site and the company would have to choose between performing in Glastonbury and continuing to employ that person. That person continued to be employed for some future years so performances in Glastonbury Abbey were not scheduled into those seasons' venue lists. Only when he had left the company were performances there happily resumed, held very successfully in the area which had been the cathedral's Choir and framed by the dramatic ruins of the North Transept. Anne benefitted hugely from the performances there as people in the Glastonbury Abbey audiences, particularly Will Parfitt and Patti Howe, helped her not only with the publicity for the plays but for academic research on their arcane significance.

In 1993 Theatre Set-Up tried, with a variety of success or disaster, to present *Hamlet* in many cathedrals around the UK. Bristol Cathedral was the first one in which the acoustic problems were revealed. The actors' dialogue was echoed by the resonant acoustics of the cathedral so that all the words seemed to be run into each other. It was a disaster, followed by similar results in Liverpool Cathedral, Hereford Cathedral (where the words could be heard properly up to only one foot from the stage area) and Salisbury Cathedral (where, however, the play looked beautiful in the setting). Audiences naturally asked for their money back and the experience left the company in considerable debt. Only the performances in Durham Cathedral, Worcester Cathedral and Southwark Cathedral were satisfactory and several performances were held there in future years.

A truly chilling frisson was felt by the actors in Germany when they first entered the auditorium of Das SchlossTheater im Neuen Palais im Park, Sanssouci, in Potsdam which had been built for Frederick the Great of Prussia. The interior of the theatre itself was magnificently golden, featuring bas reliefs and statues of musical instruments, grapes and the tall handsome young men whom Frederick admired. The seats in the auditorium were cushioned in plush red velvet, but alarmingly, the front row seats were embroidered with the Germanic heraldic symbol of the Imperial Eagle, The Reichsadler. This was last used in Germany by the Nazis and the cast knew for sure that Hitler and his cronies had sat in those seats watching a performance on the theatre's stage when he was in power!

In pleasing contrast, in the Netherlands castle of Muiderslot, Anne's favourite venue, the company's dressing room was in the study of the Dutch playwright, Pieter Hooft, a near contemporary of Shakespeare. There were pictures of scenes from his plays on the walls of rooms in the castle and the castle's custodians told the actors the context of the pictures within the plays' plots. In its relationship to the person of Pieter Hooft, the castle is for the literary heritage of the Netherlands just like the site of Shakespeare's house in Stratford-upon-Avon is significant for the past presence of Shakespeare.

Also in the Netherlands, the spectacular 14th century Loevestein Castle, where Theatre Set-Up performed for several years, held historical memories within its stout walls of the struggle of the Netherlands to overthrow their Spanish overlords. It was used as a political prison from 1619 and a plaque mounted on the walls there records the escape of herself and of her husband (the lawyer, poet and politician, Hugo de Groot) by Maria van Reigersberch by hiding in a book chest that was often sent for them. The Theatre Set-Up actors over the years of their performances there, usually grew to respect the bravery of those who had fought from its walls to establish Dutch freedom. However, there was a garderobe (an ancient species of toilet consisting of a sloping hole in the wall leading down into the moat) in the corner of the part of the castle which served as the actors' changing room. As the toilets which the actors were expected to use were a considerable distance from the changing room, one of the actors always excused himself in the garderobe, protesting that he was "getting into historical character" for the play. Anne wondered how many of the other actors were doing the same when backs were turned.

TOILETS

Toilets which were available for the audience but difficult for actors in costume to use usually forced male actors in outdoor performances to use convenient bushes near the stage site of the venue behind which to relieve themselves. Actresses usually changed into dressing gowns just before the plays' intervals and ran for the toilets which the audience were also using. Mike Nelhams, the Tresco Island head gardener, whose house was just behind the stage area where the plays were performed, made his bathroom available for the actors to use. One year when *Hamlet* was being performed, Anne who was performing the role of Queen Gertrude, was seen to enter this bathroom by the very young daughter of the household who did not know the play or its characters.

"Mummy, the Queen's in our bathroom!" she exclaimed, wondering how Her Majesty, Queen Elizabeth II had come to the island without anyone knowing about it.

That also occurred the same year when Anne in Gertrude's costume used the public toilets in Carisbrooke Castle in the Isle of Wight. A little girl waiting to use the toilet shouted to her mother who was waiting for her outside:

"Mummy, come in here quickly. The Queen's in one of the toilets!"

Sometimes the men in the audience also relieved themselves behind onsite bushes. This happened regularly in the grounds of Scotney Castle, Kent, as the toilets were up a very steep slope leading from the location of the play. One evening two men, unaware of each other's presence behind opposite sides of a bush, unwittingly became caught in each other's "crossfire". It became an anecdote of the venue.

"Crossed swords!" commented the play's event organiser.

In 1986 on the first day of the season of *The Comedy of Errors*, it was, however, an incident involving an ordinary indoor toilet in Anne's first floor flat that created a memorable opening of the tour for the plays' cast. Anne always began the season with a meeting in her flat with the cast and a discussion not only of the tour schedule and related factors but the exposition of her research into the subtext of the play. During a brief break between the different elements of this meeting, one of the actors decided to go to the toilet and she shut its door by turning its door key which promptly broke in half, leaving her locked in and unable to get out. A number of attempts were made by the stage manager to rescue her by borrowing a neighbour's ladder, placing it up to the toilet's window and encouraging her to try to climb out of the window and then come down the ladder. However the actress was too fearful of this manoeuvre to try it. He then tried unsuccessfully to force open the toilet door. Finally Anne called to the imprisoned actress:

"Just put down the toilet seat and sit on it until I fetch the fire brigade."

She phoned the fire brigade who were delighted to receive her call:

"Good morning. I am speaking on behalf of a professional theatre company. Please can you help us here. There is an actress locked in the lavatory!"

They responded to the anecdotal drama of this situation with all the resources they could summon. Six of them, dressed from head to foot in bright yellow oilskins, climbed ostentatiously into the fire engine whose bell they rang loudly all the way from the fire station to Anne's flat. Having alerted the whole district to the possibility that they were on the way to a major conflagration, they vigorously jumped down from the fire engine, following their leader who waved the instrument of rescue in the air. This was a huge jemmy which could prise open the toilet door. Entering the flat with a theatrical flourish, they all lined up along the stairway leading to the toilet, their yellow oilskins gleaming in the glow of the hall lights. Their leader placed the jemmy into the part of the door opening nearest to the door lock and they all leaned on each other in a sequence of muscular power terminating in their leader, and at his signal they all pushed simultaneously and their combined power broke the door lock. With a dramatic gesture that would have fitted a classical romantic hero, the leader opened the door and freed the very embarrassed actress. She was a very beautiful lady whose loveliness and gracious thanks to all of them ensured them that it had been all very worthwhile. This was the result that they had been anticipating. Had it been one of the male actors locked in the toilet, indubitably there would have been less enthusiastic theatricality surrounding the event!

Lacking the generosity of the firemen, several inhospitable venues, considering actors to be non-human and the plays an additional burden to their already over-busy work schedules, closed their toilets when the play was finished but before the actors had finished packing up all the gear into the van. This made actresses as well as the actors learn to make good use of nearby bushes! When the actors were treated like that, they called it the "Rogues and Vagabonds" syndrome, recalling the many years when actors were considered to be travelling criminals and often the worthies of towns where they were hoping to perform would pay them to go away!

ROGUES AND VAGABONDS

Sometime local residents of venues hosting the plays also had an unsympathetic attitude to the performances of Shakespeare's plays in their midst. At a performance in 2000 of *A Midsummer Night's Dream,* the farming neighbour of the owner of Great Bidlake Manor in Devon expressed his disapproval of the event by operating a very noisy muck-spreader all the way throughout the play in a field adjacent to the performance. This could not reasonably be objected to during the first half of the play while there was light, but the farmer made his point by continuing to do so in the second dark part of the evening, having targeted muck at the manor's owner who had entered the field during the play's interval to ask him to stop. It was impossible to create the magical atmosphere which the play demands with such noisy aggression disrupting it and the discouraged owner did not present any more plays on his property, although he subsequently pointed out to the farmer that many local people were in the audience and would give him a bad time in any way they could think of for his having spoilt their evening!

Another year when audiences were badly disturbed by the actions of local people unsympathetic to the performance being put on near them, occurred in the courtyard of The George Inn in South London which was known to have held performances of Shakespeare's plays in his own day. The National Trust, which owned the inn, promoted the performance but also kept the courtyard open for its regular clients, most of whom were surgeons from a nearby hospital. Over their much-needed drinks, these overworked medics described in gruesome detail all the surgeries that they had been obliged to perform that day, in voices unfortunately loud enough not only to be heard by each other but by the members of the audience and the actors. It was, in fact, a kind of competition between two different kinds of theatre – one medical, the other dramatic. However the surrounding audience, especially people who were squeamish, were very put off and the idea of any future productions there were abandoned.

Another evening which did not turn out as the cast had expected was the last night of performances of *Love's Labour's Lost* at Fountains Abbey in 1984. There had been a problem during the first night of *A Midsummer Night's Dream* being performed there in the previous year when the audience had heard very little of the play as the young pilots of a nearby Royal Airforce outfit decided to harass the performance by test-flying their planes low over the performance area. However help was at hand as one of the Fountains Abbey administrators was an ex-RAF member of staff. He telephoned the RAF outfit the following morning, asking to be put through to the person in charge.

"Hello C.H., M.W. speaking here. I say, last night some of your chappies..."

So the next night's performance was played beneath silent skies.

BIZARRE EVENTS

However there was no providential "Deus Ex Machina" like the ex-RAF staff member to rescue the *Love's Labour's Lost* company on one extraordinary evening in 1984 at Fountains Abbey. Anne first realised that something was wrong before the start of the performance when she came upon all the male actors looking frantically through the script of the play. They ultimately told her that one of the actors had "walked", in other words not appeared on site for the beginning of the play, having become drunk during the day and wandered off, to where nobody knew! The male actors were all seeing how they could cover this actor's roles between them and thus salvage the production that evening. Anne asked the stage manager to contact the police to trace the "walked" actor to find out if he had had an accident and to locate him while the actors sought ways to replace him.

The roles he was playing were firstly Longaville, a lord attendant to the King of Navarre and then Marcade, a messenger. Frank Jarvis, who was playing the role of Don Adriano De Armado, had added to the Spanish style of this character by attaching a flourishing moustache on his upper lip with the appropriate glue, and he realised that by taking this off for performing the role of Longaville and changing into that role's costume and then by reapplying the moustache and changing back into the Spaniard's costume, he could effect a reasonable transformation between the characters. The problem would be that considerable pain would be caused by the pulling off and reapplying the moustache with its glue, but as the senior actor in the company, he would suffer this discomfort in displaying an appropriate theatre trouper's courage. An elaborate folder cover was always kept in the props box and this would disguise to a certain extent the script which Frank would need to read from in order to say Longaville's lines in the play.

The role of Marcade was slight but important. Dressed in sombre black, his role was to disrupt the festivities of the entourages of the King of Navarre and the Princess of France to announce with a very few words that the father of the Princess had died and that she was now the Queen of France. Every other male in the company wanted to play Marcade, so it was decided that the character's costume would be set in the changing area and whoever was free at the time would get into it and play the part. When the cue came for Marcade's entrance, the actor playing Boyet, attendant on the Princess, was found to be dressed and ready to sally forth with the message. Thus the actors, in the famed "We never closed!" style, carried off the production with aplomb.

Bravely plastering his very sore top lip with a soothing ointment, Frank Jarvis climbed into the passenger seat of Anne's car ready to be driven to his home to the north of London after the performance was over and everything packed up into the company's van. Anne had discovered that the missing actor had hitched-hiked home where he had come to his senses and was predictably desolate at his unprofessional behaviour, which, but for the skilled intervention of his fellow actors, would have closed the performance, presented before an audience of over 800 people that evening!

But there was more drama to come that night. As Anne and her passenger drove along the A1 which would take them from Yorkshire to north London, there was a loud bang from a burst tyre. Fortunately Anne had an emergency triangle which she put to the right on the road behind the stopped car, but she was concerned to get Frank to a Services stop further ahead where he would be more comfortable. She got out of the car and held out her arm to try to hitch-hike a lift for him but was puzzled when any approaching cars speeded past her in seeming alarm. Finally a post office van stopped and its postman driver, as requested, took Frank on board to get him the Services, promising to call the AA on Anne's behalf from there. After some time an AA van arrived and negotiated to change the wheel of the car. Before he could do that Anne begged him to kindly drive her to the Services to see if Frank was OK and then for him to return to fix the wheel. If she found Frank to be all right she would ask the policeman they knew was always stationed at those Services to drive her back to the car. He agreed and on arrival at the Services Anne found to her relief that Frank was indeed well. In fact he had found a captive audience in the café there and was entertaining the diners with a song and dance routine!

Anne was also relieved to see the police car there, the policeman sitting in it with his window partly open, waiting to assist in any forthcoming crisis. She joyfully ran towards the car, but on seeing her, the policeman started in terror, winding up his window and staring at her in horror. Eventually she persuaded him to open his window and he ultimately succumbed to her request to drive her back to her car, hopefully with its wheel changed and thus be able to proceed forwards on the A1. This all went to plan and Anne drove Frank home with no further disasters.

When Anne arrived home she happened to look at herself in a mirror and was horrified by what she saw. Her stage makeup, which she had not had the time to remove, had become smudged and randomly spread over her face, covered with streaks of black dust from her efforts to hitch-hike a lift for Frank on the side of the A1. She looked like a mad woman! No wonder that the people in the cars racing past her and the terrified policeman were loath to have any contact with her. She subsequently found out that there was a Yorkshire legend proclaiming the presence of a monstrous ghost appearing in the region of the A1 and the Services where she had been asking for help. Evidently the people driving the cars which speeded past her and the terrified policeman had thought that this rumoured apparition was real and that she was its embodiment, and the man driving the post office van and the AA service man had either not heard of the legend or did not believe in such "nonsense". You may be sure that the next time Anne saw Frank Jarvis, she reprimanded him for not having warned her about her monstrous appearance!

However, no event in any venue could exceed the bizarre phenomena which surrounded several of the performances on Tresco in the Isles of Scilly. One of the most charming features of the performance there was the provision for the children of tourists and residents of the Scillies. A large tarpaulin was laid in the very front of the grassed audience area, and soon it was filled with dozens of excited children, all of whom were well behaved during the course of the plays, blissfully unaware that what they were seeing had been tailored to make possible the transport of the productions to that very spot.

The design of all Theatre Set-Up's productions carried the stamp upon them of the task of getting Shakespeare productions to this island on the edge of the Atlantic Ocean. The productions of the plays had to be designed each year in such a way that all the costumes and gear could be carried, bit by bit, down the steep slippery stone steps leading from the St Mary's quay into the vessel that would take the gear and the cast to Tresco Island for a performance there in the Tresco Abbey Gardens. In 1996 while it was being carried down the steps, the board displaying the photos of that year's play, *Romeo and Juliet*, slid noisily off the steps into the sea below where presumably it still lies. The backstage "green room", and main changing area for the actors was in the gardeners' open shed called "Valhalla" as on the walls of its entrance porch were attached many figure-heads from ships that had been wrecked on the coasts of the Scillies. The actors, seeing these, were very aware that however bizarre were the strange events that occurred to them on the Theatre Set-Up tours, at least, unlike the unfortunate sailors of the wrecked ships, they still had their lives!

The most extraordinary of these unusual events occurred when the island's host of Theatre Set-Up's performances on the island decided to try to arrange the shows in the manner of those of the West End of London, which mostly started at 7.30pm. This would mean that the audience would be leaving the performance area deep within the beautiful Tresco Abbey Gardens in total darkness. Inhabitants of places like the island of Tresco learn to find their way about in the dark, and scorn anyone who does not have the same ability, therefore no lighting was provided for the audience to find their way to Carn Near, a dog-legged-shaped pier nearest to the

Gardens where a commissioned launch would come to take them to the main Scillonian island of St Mary's where their accommodation was located in hotels and B&Bs. The narrow road which leads to the even narrower turn-off-left road to this pier also leads to another pier in the Tresco village of New Grimsby where commissioned launches and private boats would take the residents of other Scillonian islands to their homes there.

In the pitch dark it can be imagined what scenarios evolved from this situation. Some tourists among the audience, wishing to return to St Mary's and who at last managed to find their way out of the gardens, could not find their way to either pier but hazarded a guess that the wider road which lead to New Grimsby must be the one which would take them to the launch for St Mary's. They therefore climbed into the wrong launch and found themselves marooned on the wrong island, rescued by the locals who supplied them with tents for their compulsory overnight stay, no other launch being available until the next day for the journey back to St Mary's! A lecturer from the University of Liverpool and members of his family who had been to the Tresco performance on the first night were caught in this situation and subsequently in other mix-ups throughout their stay.

"We have slept in tents on the island of Bryher, taken refuge in the toilets on the quay of St Mary's and gone on numerous unscheduled launch journeys. Since we have encountered your theatre company we have felt that we have been living in a parallel universe!" they said to Anne when they bumped into her on St Mary's.

In later years the productions would begin at 6pm so that these problems would not occur, but the later start time for these performances that year had been advertised and a solution had to be found. So the Tresco Abbey gardeners decided that they would bend to the needs of tourists in the audience by placing night lights in dozens of empty jam jars which they would put along the way out from the audience area in the Garden and then along the roads leading to Carn Near pier. When they did this it looked magical and Anne decided that, although she had accommodation available on Tresco, she should follow the audience along this fairy-tale route to monitor exactly what would happen to the people from the audience.

It was so dark that no-one recognised her as she joined all the people hoping to find their way back to their accommodation on St Mary's. They all shuffled their way cautiously along the dog-legged Carn Near pier and waited in pitch black darkness for the anticipated launch to arrive.

"We've been conned," said one man, "There's nothing in sight!"

After about 10 minutes the welcome lights of an approaching launch glimmered towards them. On its arrival they all gratefully clambered aboard it, but there was a problem on the arrival of the launch in St Mary's. It was so late at night that all the loaded fishing boats had come in and were stretched in a long queue behind the first of them to have arrived there. This boat had been able to be anchored beside the steps of the quay. Protocol and necessity decreed that all following boats and launches should take their places in orderly fashion in this queue which meant that the launch from Tresco was the last in line and its passengers would have to climb over each boat in turn until they reached the steps of the quay to which the first boat was anchored. Thus the audience members had the unique but perilous post-theatre experience of climbing from rocking boat to rocking boat over catches of slippery fish lying with glazed eyes looking sightlessly up at them.

Among these astounded people was a shivering American couple who were so traumatised by the effort to get to the shore that Anne had to phone one of her friends to come to drive them to their hotel.

In their distress they seemed to sum up the extraordinary nature of Theatre Set-Up's performances of Shakespeare in heritage sites.

"Oh my God. We don't go to the theatre in the States like this!" they cried.

"It's not normal in this country," responded Anne.

ILLUSTRATIONS

COVER PHOTO.
Rosalind Cressy as
Cleopatra, Tony
Portacio as Antony
in *Antony and
Cleopatra*.
Photo: Wendy and
Michael Gains

FIG. 1. *All's Well
that Ends Well*, 1990,
Forty Hall, Enfield.
Proteus (Tony
Portacio), Parolles
(Frank Jarvis),
Duke of Florence
(Michael Palmer).

FIG. 2. *Much Ado About Nothing*, 1981 Performed against the front façade of Chiswick House. Later productions were staged in the Temple Amphitheatre.

FIG. 3. *Much Ado About Nothing*, 1999, Kedlestone Hall, Derby.

FIG. 4. *Much Ado About Nothing*, 1981, The Orangery, Saltram House.
Benedick (Frank Jarvis), Beatrice (Susannah Best).

FIG. 5. *As you Like It*, 1980, Tresco Abbey Gardens.
Duke Senior (David Eadon), Le Beau (Paul Fortey).

FIG. 6. The auditorium with candelabra lit, Slot Loevestein, The Netherlands.

FIG. 7. *The Tempest*, 1982, Stonehenge, Wiltshire.

FIG. 8. *The Taming of the Shrew,* 1994. Petruchio (Tony Portacio), Katharine (Libby Machin) wearing the red wig subsequently stolen by a fox in the following year's production of *A Midsummer Night's Dream.*

FIG. 9. Actors swimming at night (against the wishes of the Theatre Set-Up management Risk Assessment factors) in the Hardanger Fjord, Norway, 2004.

111

FIG. 10. While the audience wait behind the gate, the Baroniet Rosendal
staff set up the courtyard wet-weather arrangements, 1994.

FIG. 11. The first night banquet, Baroniet Rosendal, 1993.

FIG. 12. *The Tempest*, 1982. Costumes with masks for spirits conjured up by Ariel. (Henrietta and Michael Bramwell).

FIG. 13. *Much Ado About Nothing*, 1981. Wendy Macphee as musician in "The Lampshade", a fringed Victorian dress, with the portable antique organ.

FIG. 14. *The Tempest*, 1982, Scotney Castle. Actor preparing "backstage left" before the Theatre Set-Up provision of changing tents in 1993.

FIG. 15. *Romeo and Juliet*, 1996, Forty Hall. The Friar (with Michael Palmer correctly wearing the friar's costume), Juliet (Victoria Stillwell), Romeo (Neil Warhurst).

FIG. 16. *A Midsummer Night's Dream*, 1983, Forty Hall. Derek Crewe as Starveling performing "Moonshine" with the wooden dog which was later thrown into the carp pond at Sudeley Castle.

FIG. 17. *As You Like It* 1980, Scotney Castle. Lutenist (Wendy Macphee), Rosalind (Susannah Best), Phoebe (Caroline Funnell).

FIG. 18. *The Two Gentlemen of Verona* 1987, Cotehele on an unusually dry evening. Photo: The Western Morning News.

FIG. 19. *The Tempest* 1982, Scotney Castle. Prospero (Robert MacLeod), Miranda (Elizabeth Stanley), Ferdinand (Ben Benson), Ariel (Antony Taylor).

FIG. 20. *Hamlet* 1993, in the mountain and fjord Norwegian setting of
The Baroniet of Rosendal. Marcellus (Matthew Rixon).

FIG. 21. *Twelfth Night* 1979, The Rose Garden, Forty Hall. Olivia (Caroline Funnell), Viola (Susannah Best).

FIG. 22. "Daffodil" the company van in 1981, towing gear in "Marigold". In later years these were replaced by a two-year old high top Mercedes Benz Sprinter van which comfortably carried all the costumes and gear and five actors. A car carried a further two or three actors.

APPENDIX I

A tribute to the talent and rigour of some of the Theatre Set-Up actors exemplified in their work following their seasons with the company. This is a conservative account of these actors' accomplishments. Most actors perform in some films and TV in addition to their stage work so that is assumed as part of the C.V.s of the actors in all the lists.

1. **Maintaining theatre work in the UK, often serving the needs of local communities and performing in repertory and regional theatres as well as London mainstream, and in fringe and outdoor locations**
    Terry Ashe, Richard Ashley, Mark Bodicoat, James Clarkson, Sean Chapman, Alan Collins, Andrew Crabb, Jonathan Gunning, David Holmes, Peter Landi, Tim Lowe, Peter Lundie Wager, James Morley, Daniel O'Brien, Deborah O'Malley, Emily Outred, Paul Rainbow, Anthony Taylor, Richard Plumley, Simon Startin, Kyra Williams.

2. **In addition to performing in the UK, acting/directing/producing outside the UK**
    Sean Aita (Europe), Elizabeth Arends (USA), Sue Appleby (world tour), Susannah Best (world tour), Paul Brennan (China), Morag

Brownlie (Europe), Kim Evans (Europe), Andrew Field (Europe), Simon Furness (Europe), Jonathan Hartman (Canada and USA), Tim Heath (Europe), Ciaran Hinds (world tour), Jenni Lea-Jones (Europe), Libby Machin (Middle East), Alex Marshall (Europe), Jo Price (USA), Emma Reynolds (Europe), Christopher Terry (world tour).

3. **Establishing their own companies**

Sean Aita, Iain Armstrong, Susannah Best, Henrietta and Michael Branwell, Morag Brownlie, Rosalind Cressy, James Kingdon, Alexa Jago, Angela Laverick, Libby Machin, Chris Pavlo, David Reakes.

4. **Writing – books and scripts for stage and TV**

Sean Aita, Jack Hughes, Deborah O'Malley, Anita Parry, Chris Pavlo, Stewart Permutt, Chris Robbie, Emma Reynolds, Simon Startin, Tim Heath, Neil Warhurst, Anthony Young.

5. **Teaching – voice, drama, workshops, in theatres, drama schools, university and schools**

Sean Aita (university professor), Susannah Best (international workshops for the British Council), Alison Breminer (voice and text coach RSC), Mark Bodicoat (Schools), Henrietta and Michael Branwell (ballet – to own company in Harlow and Pineapple, Morley College and Central School of Ballet in London), Lucy Curtin (varied venues), Tess Dignan (voice and text coach RSC), David Eadon (Schools), Kim Evans (schools), Gordon Fleming (acting instruction to ballet dancers), Simon Furness (varied venues), Melanie Jessop (voice and drama coach/ tutor/ director in drama schools including RADA and Webber Douglas), Michael Loney (Arts establishments, Australia), David Norell (schools), Michael Palmer (tutor, drama schools),

Tony Portacio (schools), George Richmond-Scott (voice and text coach RSC).

6. **Performing in the National Theatre**
Charles Abomali, Sean Aita, Lynette Edwards, Guy Henry, Ciaran Hinds, Fabian Cartwright, Julie Le Grand, Deborah O'Malley, Simon Startin.

7. **Performing in the Royal Shakespeare Company**
Charles Abomali, Sean Aita, Sean Chapman, Simon Clerk, Derek Crewe, Steven Elder, Guy Henry, Ciaran Hinds, Sarah-Jane Holm, Melanie Jessop, Julie Le Grand, Matthew Rixon, Chris Robbie.

8. **Diversified within theatre in addition to stage/TV/film**
Julia Ackerman (voice overs), Sean Chapman (voice overs), Susie Coleman (voice overs), Suzie Edwards (role playing), Caroline Funnell (casting director, UK and Europe), David Goudge (radio), Tim Heath (director), Kevin Howarth (horror movies actor), Daniel Hunt (director), Alexa Jago (executive film director), Frank Jarvis (director), Chris Jordan (director/producer/theatre manager), Hugh Kermode (radio/creative director), Michael Loney (marriage celebrant Australia), James Mitchell (magic), Peter O'Dwyer (producer), Geoffrey Owen (performance coach), Anita Parry (artistic director), Chris Pavlo (executive director, radio), Jacqueline Quella (executive producer of major events, film and other media), Emma Reynolds (voice over, direction), Alex Richardson (film director), Amanda Strevett-Smith (drama therapy), Elliot Tiney (stand-up comedian), David Wylde (role play – in addition to drama school teaching).
After her performances in the West End, Victoria Stillwell (who had played Juliet in our 1996 production of "Romeo and Juliet"), became an animal behaviour expert specialising in dogs, with her

own business and TV shows in the UK and the USA. Particularly famous was the TV series, "It's Me or the Dog" (see above p. 287). She took the precaution of warning Anne of this in case she should suffer shock at unexpectedly seeing her in this capacity on her TV screen. Sean Chapman (who played Benvolio in the Theatre Set-Up 1978 production of "Romeo and Juliet"), was the narrator in some of those episodes.

APPENDIX II

Venues in which Theatre Set-Up performed during their seasons from 1976 to 2011.

1. **In the UK, the Channel Islands and the Isle of Man:**
   Abbotsbury SubTropical Garden, Dorset; Albury Park, Surrey; Alnwick Castle, Northumberland; Appleby Castle, Cumberland; Arlington Court, North Devon; Arreton Manor, Isle of Wight; Beningbrough Hall, Yorkshire; Bicton Park, Devon; Binchester Roman Fort, County Durham; Blickling Hall, Norfolk; Bowhill Country Park, Scottish Borders; Broadlands, Hampshire; The Bothey, Avenue House Grounds, London N3; The Bridgwater Amphitheatre, Lakeside Arts Centre, Nottingham; Bristol Cathedral; Broxbourne Civic Hall Gardens, Hoddesdon; Buckden Towers, Cambridgeshire; Carisbrooke Castle, Isle of Wight; Carlisle Cathedral; Castle Rushen High School; The Chaplaincy, St Mary's Isles of Scilly; Chatley Heath Semaphore Tower, Cobham, Surrey; Chatsworth House Gardens, Derbyshire; Corfe Castle, Dorset; Corn Exchange, Bury St Edmunds; Cossington Manor Gardens, Somerset; Cotehele, Cornwall; Cricket St Thomas, Somerset; The Crush Room, Royal Opera House; Dilston Castle, Northumberland; Dunster Castle,

Somerset; Durham Cathedral; Dyrham Park, near Bath; Ely Cathedral; Erddig Garden, Wales; The Evesham Festival; Fenton House, Hampstead, London; Forty Hall, Enfield; Ford Park, Cumbria; Fountains Abbey, North Yorkshire; Fountain Garden, Westmere, Birmingham; The Glade in the Forest, Rosliston Forestry Centre, Derbyshire; Grand Square, Royal Naval College, Greenwich; Great Bidlake Manor, Devon; Great Garden, Nash's House & New Place, Stratford-upon-Avon; The Greater London Theatre, County Hall, London SE1; The George Inn, Southwark, London SE1; The Georgian Theatre Royal, Richmond, North Yorkshire; Glastonbury Abbey, Somerset; Guildhall, Bath; Hall's Croft, Stratford-upon-Avon; Hanbury Hall, Worcestershire; Harlow Carr Botanical Gardens, Harrogate; Hatfield House Gardens, Hertfordshire; Heathfield Walled Garden, Croydon; Hereford Cathedral; Holland Park Open Air Theatre, London; Holme Pierrepont Hall, Nottingham; Hutton-in-the-Forest, Penrith; Ingatestone Hall, Essex; Kedleston Hall, Derbyshire; Kenilworth Castle, Warwickshire; Kentwell Hall, Suffolk; Killerton Gardens, Exeter, Devon; Kirby Hall, Northampton; Kirby Muxloe Castle, Leicerstershire; Lacock Abbey, Wiltshire; Lamport Hall, Gardens, Northamptonshire; La Seigneurie, Sark, Channel Islands; Liverpool Cathedral; The Lost Gardens of Heligan, Cornwall; Marble Hill, Richmond, London; The Medieval Hall, The Cathedral Close, Salisbury; Millfield Theatre, Edmonton London N18; Milntown, Isle of Man; Mont Orgueil, Jersey, Channel Islands; Mottisfont Abbey, Romsey; Mount Edgecumbe House and Park, Cornwall; The National Trust, Sutton Hoo, Suffolk; Norwich Cathedral; The Noverre Suite, The Assembly Rooms, Norwich; Oakhill Park Arena, London EN4; The Orangery, The Royal Botanical Gardens Kew; The Orangery, Kenwood, London NW3; Pavilion Theatre, Brighton; Peel Castle, Isle of Man; Pencarrow, Cornwall; Pendennis Castle, Cornwall; Penlanole Living Willow Theatre, Wales;

Plas Newyd, Wales; Priors Hall Barn, Essex; Penshurst Place, Kent; Peterborough Cathedral Cloisters; Powderham Castle, Devon; The Pump Room, Bath; Production Village OpenAir Theatre, London NW2; Rangers House, Black Heath, London SE10; Ripon Cathedral; Richmond Castle, North Yorkshire; The River Gardens, Pembroke Arms Hotel, Wilton, Wiltshire; The Roman Theatre, Verulamium, St Albans; The Rookery, Streatham Common, London SW4; Rothley Court, Leicester; Royal William Yard, Plymouth; Rushen Abbey, Isle of Man; St. Andrew's Church, Plymouth; St Gabriel's Church, Cwmbran, Wales; Salisbury Cathedral; Saltram House, Devon; Scotney Castle, Kent; La Seigneurie, Sark; Southwark Cathedral; Speeds Farm, Shepton Mallett; Speke Hall, Liverpool; "Starveacres", Radlet; Stonehenge, Wiltshire; Stourhead, Wiltshire; Stokesay Castle, South Shropshire; Sudbury Hall, Derbyshire; Sudeley Castle, Cheltenham; Sun Pavilion, Valley Gardens, Harrogate; Sutton Park, North Yorkshire; Tatton Park Old Hall, Knutsford, Cheshire; Theatre Royal, Bury St Edmunds, Suffolk; Temple Amphitheatre, Chiswick House Gardens, London W4; The Tivoli Theatre, Wimborne Minster; Trelissick Garden, Cornwall; Tresco Abbey, Tresco, Isles of Scilly; Trevarno, Helston, Cornwall; Tewkesbury Abbey; Upstairs at the Gatehouse, Highgate, London N6; Ventnor Botanic Garden, Isle of Wight; Wallington, Northumberland; Wenlock Priory, Much Wenlock, Shropshire; Wesley Memorial Church, Oxford; Weston Park, Shropshire; Witley Court Grounds, Worcestershire; Winchester Cathedral; Wollaton Hall, Nottingham; Worcester Cathedral. (138)

2. **In mainland Europe:**
"Arkadenhof", Rheinische Friedrich-Wilhelms-Universität Bonn, Germany; Baroniet Rosendal, Norway; Biekorf Theaterzaal, Brugge, Belgium; Château De Prangins, Geneva,

Switzerland; Château De Waleffe, Belgium; De Groenzaal, Gent; Das SchlossTheater im Neuen Palais im Park, Sanssouci, Potsdam, Germany; De Nieuwe Kerk, Dam, Amsterdam, The Netherlands; Domein De Renesse, Belgium; Glimmingehus, Sweden; Gravensteen, Gent; "Hof des Alten Schlosses", Württembergisches Landesmuseum, Stuttgart, Germany; Kasteel Ammersoyen, The Netherlands; Kasteel Doorwerth, The Netherlands; Königsaal, Schloss Heidelberg, Germany; Landcommanderij, Alden Biesen, Bilzen, Belgium; Muiderslot, The Netherlands; Rijksmuseum Gevangenpoort, Den Haag, The Netherlands; Salle Paroissiale, Limpertsberg, Luxembourg; Sarajevo The MSS Festival; Slot Loevestein, The Netherlands; Stadsschouwburg Koninklijke, Brugge, Belgium; Stadthalle Offenburg, Germany; Teatermuseet I Hofteatret, Copenhagen, Denmark; Ten Weyngaert VZW Brussels, Belgium.

Printed in Great Britain
by Amazon

13947799R00078